# Hebrews

*A Digest of Reformed Comment*

# Hebrews

*A Digest of Reformed Comment*

## GEOFFREY B. WILSON

MINISTER OF BIRKBY BAPTIST CHURCH

HUDDERSFIELD

THE BANNER OF TRUTH TRUST

# THE BANNER OF TRUTH TRUST

78b Chiltern Street, London WIM IPS

\*

© 1970 *Geoffrey B. Wilson*

First published 1970

\*

*Printed in Great Britain by*
*Hazell Watson & Viney Ltd*
*Aylesbury, Bucks*

TO MY MOTHER AND IN MEMORY OF
MY FATHER

# CONTENTS

# CONTENTS

# PREFACE

As this book was produced under the conviction that nothing is truly devotional which is not wholly scriptural, it is hoped that it may arouse feelings in the reader which can be rightly called Christian because they are the fruit of serious reflection upon the Word of God.

I would like to express my thanks to the publishers of the various works quoted for their generous co-operation, and I am especially grateful to Professor F. F. Bruce who kindly permitted me to make free use of his valuable commentary on this Epistle.

Geoffrey Wilson.

Huddersfield.
January, 1970.

# INTRODUCTION

It is certain that the first readers of this Epistle knew its author, but this knowledge has been lost to posterity because he did not put his name to it. Consequently the identity of the writer remains one of the unsolved mysteries of New Testament introduction. Its attribution to the Apostle Paul is more convenient than convincing, and the many modern attempts to find a more credible alternative to the Pauline authorship have signally failed to pierce this baffling veil of anonymity. However, the providential suppression of the name of its human author is evidently intended to focus attention upon the divine origin of the message itself. When God is acknowledged as the real speaker it is of no consequence if a particular voice he chooses to use cannot be recognized. [*Heb.* 1:1]

It is almost as great a problem to determine the identity of those addressed by the writer. Some scholars have suggested that it was intended for Gentile readers, but the argument of the letter strongly supports the traditional belief that it was sent to Hebrew Christians, even though its destination is still a matter of conjecture. It was probably written shortly before the fall of Jerusalem in A.D. 70, when the sacrificial system was abruptly terminated by the destruction of the temple.

This 'word of exhortation' was made necessary by the failure of these Jewish believers to grasp the real significance of the Person and Work of Christ. They must understand that those ceremonies under which the gospel was typically set

[11]

forth in former days have been superseded by the advent of Him in whom they have found their perfect fulfilment. That priesthood in which men 'were not suffered to continue by reason of death' has been abolished by the once-for-all redemptive accomplishment of Christ who is a priest 'for ever after the order of Melchisedec.' For when the true glory of Christ's heavenly Priesthood is discerned all earthly pretensions to the sacerdotal office must be abandoned.

# CHAPTER ONE

*V*1: **God, who at sundry times and in divers manners spake in time past unto the fathers by the prophets,**

*V*2: **Hath in these last days spoken unto us by his Son, whom he hath appointed heir of all things, by whom also he made the worlds;**

*V*3: **Who being the brightness of his glory, and the express image of his person, and upholding all things by the word of his power, when he had by himself purged our sins, sat down on the right hand of the Majesty on high;**

In this sublime announcement of the Epistle's theme its author is not merely reminding those who had been privileged to receive the divine oracles of the undisputed fact that God had spoken unto the fathers, but he rather seeks to underline the preparatory and progressive character of that revelation. In former days God spoke to Israel 'in the prophets' (RV) at various times and in a great variety of ways. These men were not free to interpret the message they had received from God in words of their own choosing, for the divine afflatus under which they spoke extended to the very words they uttered. [2 *Pet* 1:21] Geerhardus Vos makes the following comment on the significance of the preposition which is used here: 'To say that God was speaking in the prophets need not detract at all from their intelligence, but it does serve to emphasize the absolute character of the resultant prophecies. We need not be concerned so much about the *processes* of revelation, provided we maintain a firm conviction that the *product* of revelation is truly the infallible Word of God. This we find in Hebrews, which lays strong stress on the fact that the revelation was *in* the prophets.'

There is general unbelief in the Word of God because it is commonly mistaken for a purely human word which men may reject with impunity. Micaiah cannot have spoken God's word for his testimony was not acceptable to Ahab, and Jehoiakim burnt the message he took for the pessimistic utterance of an exceedingly troublesome prophet, but God vindicated His word, and incidentally His servants, in the judgment which overtook those who opposed it. [1 *Kings* 22; *Jer* 36] However, that which sinners use as an excuse for their repudiation of Scripture is in fact the mark of its gracious character. It is for our safety that God veils His glory and sends His word to us through His servants the prophets who speak as we are able to hear it. For when God did speak directly to the children of Israel they had no doubt that it was God who spoke to them, but they were so terrified by it that 'they said unto Moses, Speak thou with us, and we will hear: but let not God speak with us, lest we die.' [*Exod* 20:19] Those who now stoutly refuse to hear Moses and the prophets will believe their testimony one day, for there are no agnostics in hell. [*Luke* 16: 19–31] It is therefore spiritual suicide to neglect that Word which was written by human hands, but which is nevertheless the veritable speech of the Living God addressed to our hearts. 'No matter whether written by Moses, the Prophets, or the Apostles of our Lord and Saviour, the one subject of the Bible is the Man Christ Jesus, "who is over all, God blessed for ever." [*Rom* 9:5] The testimony of Jesus is the spirit of prophecy, therefore thus saith the Lord Himself, "Search the Scriptures," for Moses wrote of Me, David wrote of Me, the Prophets wrote of Me, and they are they which testify of ME.' (Brownlow North, *The Rich Man and Lazarus*, p. 108)

**Hath at the end of these days spoken unto us in a Son,**
(RV margin). It was at the end of these days of Messianic expectation that God spoke His last word 'unto us' in His Son. Christ's fulfilment of Israel's ancestral hope not only brought to an end the period of promise, but also marked the beginning of 'the age to come.' These Hebrew believers could only contemplate a return to the tangible ceremonies of the Levitical system because they had completely failed to grasp the distinctive character of the dispensation in which they were now living. Such a lack of spiritual discernment always leads to the same result, for where ignorance concerning the purpose of Christ's coming prevails, a relapse into some form of ritualism becomes inevitable. In former times God spoke unto the fathers 'in *the* prophets,' but now He has spoken 'unto us in *a* Son.' The essential Deity of Him who is by nature a Son is here underlined by the omission of the definite article. It is the transcendent dignity of the One through whom this final revelation is made which emphasizes the great responsibility of those who are the recipients of it. 'But last of all he sent unto them his son.' [*Matt* 21:37] After sending His own Son, God had no one else to send. Thus Christ is God's last word to man.

'In opposition to this *gradual revelation* of the mind of God under the Old Testament, the apostle intimates that now by Jesus, the Messiah, the Lord hath at once begun and finished the whole revelation of his will, according to their own hopes and expectation. So, *Jude* 3, the faith was "once delivered unto the saints;" not in *one day*, not in *one sermon*, or by *one person*, but at *one season*, or under one dispensation, comprising all the time from the entrance of the Lord Christ upon his ministry to the closing of the canon of Scripture; which period was now at hand. This season being once past and finished, no new revelation is to be expected, to the end of the world. Nothing shall be added unto nor altered in the worship of God any more. God will not do it; men that attempt it, do it on the price of their souls.' (John Owen)

Since those addressed were faltering in their profession of faith because they entertained an inadequate view of Christ, their instructor immediately corrects this basic error by setting forth His unique glory in seven majestic assertions. The pre-eminence of the Son guarantees the superiority of that revelation which is mediated to mankind solely through Him. In these days when the propagandists from the cults aggressively hawk their spurious wares from door to door, it is vital for us to realize that a truncated Christology forms the foundation of all false teaching, and that it never fails to produce a deformed Christianity. [2 John 7–11]

### whom he hath appointed heir of all things,

1. This is the Father's eternal appointment of the Son as the mediatorial heir of the universe. The future universal recognition of Christ's sovereignty over the whole of the created order cannot fail to be realized because it is the subject of this divine decree. [Ps 2:8; Phil 2:9–11]

'His *heirship* follows His *sonship*, and preceded His *making the worlds* [Prov 8:22–23; Eph 3:11].' (A. R. Fausset) As grace promises all believers a share in this dominion, John Trapp quaintly exhorts, 'Be married to this heir, and have all!' [Rom 8:17]

### through whom also he made the worlds; (RV)

2. Next, it is explicitly affirmed that the universe was given its existence by the Son's fulfilment of the Father's creative fiat. J. B. Lightfoot draws attention to the fact that the Alexandrian Jew, Philo, commonly used the same preposition, 'through' (DIA), to describe the purely passive and instrumental rôle which he assigned to the Logos (the Word) in the work of creation. However, if the writers of the New Testament adopted Philo's language, both here and in *John* 1:3, they cer-

tainly discarded his thought, for in Scripture the Eternal Word is represented as the 'co-operating agent' in the creation of the universe. (*Commentary on Colossians and Philemon*, p. 155 on *Col* 1:16) The word which is translated in this verse as 'worlds,' usually means 'ages' (RV margin), and this suggests the further thought that Christ continues to uphold and direct 'the universe, including all space and ages, and all material and spiritual existences.' (A. R. Fausset) None but the Lord of the ages could comfort his followers with the assurance, 'Lo, I am with you alway, even unto the consummation of the age.' [*Matt* 28:20 RV margin]

## Who being the effulgence of his glory, (RV)

3. Whereas the previous statements described the splendour of the Son in terms of the Father's decree, in this verse there is a portrayal of what the Son is in His own nature. Here we are told that all the brightness of God shines forth from Him who is the very 'radiance of his glory.' (Arndt-Gingrich) The divine glory which once rested upon the 'tent of meeting' has been fully manifested in the Incarnate Word who 'tabernacled among us,' 'full of grace and truth.' [*John* 1:14. RV margin] 'Among the many causes of the extreme attachment of the Jews to the Mosaic economy, this was no doubt one, that such splendid displays of the Divine majesty had been made in connection with it; but the Apostle points them to *the glory that excelleth*, and intimates to them, that humble as was the external appearance of Jesus of Nazareth, He was the true Shekinah, in whom dwelt the Godhead bodily – the real, substantial, adequate representation of the King eternal, immortal, and invisible, whom no eye hath seen, or can see.' (John Brown)

## and the impress of his substance, (RV margin)

4. This phrase shows that the Son 'is both personally distinct from, and yet literally equal to, Him of whose essence He is the adequate imprint.' (Liddon quoted by Vine) [2 *Cor* 4:4; *Col* 1:

15] As Calvin observes, the term 'reminds us that God is known truly and firmly only in Christ. His likeness is not just veiled and concealed, but is an express image which represents God Himself, just as a coin bears the image of the die-stamp from which it is struck.' Although we cannot 'by searching find out God,' yet He is perfectly revealed to us through Him who said, 'he that hath seen me hath seen the Father.' [*Job* 11: 7; *John* 14:9]

### and upholding all things by the word of his power,

5. This impressive declaration attributes to the Son the guiding of all things in the universe to their appointed goal. 'Christ is therefore represented as the *Author of providence* in the broadest sense. To say that He does this *by the word of his power* amounts to an attestation of His *divine* power.' (G. Vos) [*Col* 1:16–17]

'This abundantly discovers the vanity and folly of them who make use of the creation in an opposition unto the Lord Christ and his peculiar interest in this world. His own power is the very ground that they stand upon in their opposition unto him, and all things which they use against him consist in him. They hold their lives absolutely at the pleasure of him whom they oppose; and they act against him without whose continual supportment and influence they could neither live nor act one moment: which is the greatest madness and most contemptible folly imaginable.' (John Owen)

### when he had by himself purged our sins,

6. The setting of this statement shows that it is impossible to grasp the meaning of the atonement unless it is seen within the context of eternity. The scandal of the Cross is only removed when it is realized that Christ suffered 'by the determinate counsel and foreknowledge of God,' and that He did this to make purification of sins. Thus our apprehension of the essential glory of the Mediator will be the measure of our

CHAPTER I VERSE 4

glorying in the Cross. This 'is sacrificial language: it points out
the objective effect of Christ's atonement. It cannot be referred
to inner renewing, because, as the past participle here shows, it
was consummated before His ascension. He did not merely
announce the purification in word; He effected it, as the terms
of the expression prove, by His sole activity, – that is, within
the sphere of His own personal action. In other words, the
apostle declares that Christ effected a purification of sin by
Himself; or, according to Levitical nomenclature, that He was
at once priest and victim – priest to offer the sacrifice, and
victim to bear the sin, here considered as a defilement that
must be purged away.' (George Smeaton)

**sat down on the right hand of the Majesty on high;**
7. Upon the completion of His atoning work Christ sat down
in the place of supreme dignity and power as the enthroned
Priest-King of His people. [*Ps* 110:1] 'As He is to be loved because of His redemption, He is also to be worshipped in this
majesty.' (Calvin)

*V*4: **Being made so much better than the angels, as he
hath by inheritance obtained a more excellent name
than they.**

**Having become by so much better than the angels, as he
hath inherited a more excellent name than they.** (RV)
The author now begins a series of comparisons in order to
prove that the superiority of the New Covenant resides in the
excellence of the Mediator through whom it is inaugurated.
Although this verse refers to Christ's Sonship as the Messiah,
His fitness to fulfil this function rests upon that essential dignity which He always possessed as the Son of God. (*v* 2)
Christ's eternal ascendancy over the angelic hosts was apparently eclipsed during the 'incomprehensible intermezzo'[1]
of His passion, but His absolute supremacy over them was

[1] H. Ridderbos, *The Coming of the Kingdom*, p. 463.

openly demonstrated when He entered into the Messianic inheritance, and 'sat down on the right hand of the Majesty on high' as the triumphant Son of Man. [*Heb* 1:3; 2:7, 9] Throughout this chapter 'the angels are not compared with Christ merely as exalted creatures, but also as revealers and administrators, in which respects also Christ is superior to them.' (G. Vos) In the giving of the law to Israel God was separated from man by a double mediation – by angelic intermediaries and by Moses – but in hailing Jesus as our 'Emmanuel' we gratefully recognize that in the gospel God Himself has stepped alongside us in the glorious person of His only begotten Son. [*Deut* 33:2; *Ps* 68:17; *Matt* 1:23; *Acts* 7:53; *Gal* 3:19] The favourite adjective of the writer appears here for the first time, though it is not difficult 'to see behind the apologetic better the dogmatic best.'[1] [*Heb* 1:4; 6:9; 7:7, 19, 22; 8:6 (twice); 9:23; 10:34; 11:16, 35, 40; 12:24].

*V5*: **For unto which of the angels said he at any time, Thou art my Son, this day have I begotten thee? And again, I will be to him a Father, and he shall be to me a Son?**

**For unto which of the angels said he at any time, Thou art my Son, this day have I begotten thee?**
This is the first of seven citations from the Old Testament which are introduced to substantiate the foregoing assertion. Here the interrogative form demands a negative reply, for what is predicated of the Son in *Psalm* 2:7 is never attributed to the angels in Scripture. On this John Owen makes the significant observation, 'An argument, then, taken negatively from the authority of the Scripture in matters of faith, or what relates to the worship of God, is valid and effectual, and here consecrated for ever to the use of the church by the apostle.' Thus the silence of Scripture affords no licence for the prac-

[1] A. B. Bruce, quoted by T. Hewitt, *The Epistle to the Hebrews*, p. 41.

tice of those rites and ceremonies which owe their origin to
the sinful imaginations of men rather than to the positive commandment of God. [*Is* 8:20] Angels are collectively referred to
as the 'sons of God' in the Old Testament, 'but *Son* is singular
to Christ, and incommunicable to any other.' (Poole) [*Job* 38:
7] 'This day' has no reference to the eternal generation of the
Son, an interpretation which Calvin quite rightly dismissed as
a 'subtlety', but rather points to the particular time when
Christ's claim to divine Sonship was decisively vindicated.
Since the Resurrection marked the beginning of Christ's exaltation, it makes no material difference whether the fulfilment
of this prophecy is referred to that event, as it is in *Acts* 13:33,
or whether it is applied to the pre-eminence of the Ascended
Christ, as it is here and in *ch* 5:5. (*v* 4). For as John Murray has
well said on *Romans* 1:4, 'Everything antecedent in the incarnate life of our Lord moves toward the resurrection and
everything subsequent rests upon it and is conditioned by it.'
(*The Epistle to the Romans*, p. 12)

**And again, I will be to him a Father, and he shall be to
me a Son?** The second testimony which could never be
ascribed to angels is taken from 2 *Samuel* 7:14 and respects the
promise which God made to David concerning the establishment of the kingdom under his son Solomon, but it is evident
that the primary fulfilment of this oracle did not exhaust its
meaning. It also spoke prophetically of the Father's relation to
the Messianic Son who 'was made of the seed of David according to the flesh.' [*Rom* 1:4] As 'the eternal and natural relation
that is between the Father and Son' cannot be the subject of a
promise, John Owen therefore explains the verse in the following way. 'If it be asked on what account God would thus
be a father unto Jesus Christ in this peculiar manner, it must
be answered that the radical, fundamental cause of it lay in the
relation that was between them from his eternal generation;
but he *manifested* himself to be his father, and engaged to deal

with him in the love and care of a father, as he had accomplished his work of mediation on the earth and was exalted unto his throne and rule in heaven.'

*V6*: **And again, when he bringeth in the firstbegotten into the world, he saith, And let all the angels of God worship him.**

**And when he again bringeth in the firstborn into the world** (RV) The supporters of the translation favoured by the RV refer the verse to the second advent, but as the evidence for this is not conclusive it is better to adhere to the AV where 'again' simply signifies the bringing forth of a further proof, this time apparently from *Deut* 32:43 LXX, though the same thought is also found in *Psalm* 97:7 LXX. It is the constant aim of the writer to make his readers realize that the age to come began with the heavenly investiture of Christ, and it is the present subjection of the inhabited earth to the sovereignty of the exalted Mediator which made such a change in worship necessary. Thus the worship which the angels were commanded to pay to Jehovah under the old economy is henceforth transferred to Christ as the 'firstborn' of God's new creation, a term which indicates His 'supreme rank and Lordship'[1] over all things. [*Col* 1:15] It should be particularly noted that it was God the Father who instituted this change in worship, for He does not promise 'to accept any thing but what is of his own appointment; so that it is the greatest folly imaginable to undertake any thing in his worship and service but what his appointment gives warrant for.' (John Owen) The verse reveals the foolishness of those who would withdraw their allegiance from the One whom even the angels worship, for 'whatever diversity of opinion there may be among men as to worshipping Christ Jesus, there is obviously but one mind and one heart in heaven.' (John Brown)

---

[1] W. Manson, *The Epistle to the Hebrews*, p. 92.

**$V$7: And of the angels he saith, Who maketh his angels spirits, and his ministers a flame of fire.**

Or **Who maketh his angels winds** (RV). In this citation from *Psalm* 104:4 the word 'maketh' underlines the inferiority of the angels to the Son. 'He is the Son; they are the creatures of God. *Only begotten* is the description of His mode of existence; *made* is the description of theirs. *All* their powers are communicated powers; and however high they may stand in the scale of creation, it is in that scale they stand, which places them infinitely below Him, who is so the Son of God as to be "God over all, blessed for ever."'(John Brown) This graphic description of the angels' service does not imply any transformation of their essence, but rather suggests that 'they are clothed with God's powers to accomplish His will in the realm of nature.' (T. Hewitt)

**$V$8: But unto the Son he saith, Thy throne, O God, is for ever and ever; a sceptre of righteousness is the sceptre of thy kingdom.**

**$V$9: Thou hast loved righteousness, and hated iniquity; therefore God, even thy God, hath anointed thee with the oil of gladness above thy fellows.**

The creaturely obedience of the angels is now contrasted with the divine sovereignty of the Son in this fifth quotation, which is from *Psalm* 45:6, 7. John Owen vigorously rejects the opinion that the psalm was composed to celebrate Solomon's marriage to Pharaoh's daughter, since the Holy Ghost could by no means endorse such a sinful union, and also because its subject matter is quite inappropriate. He concludes, 'As all, then, grant that the Messiah is *principally*, so there is no cogent reason to prove that he is not *solely*, intended in this psalm.'

**But unto the Son he saith, Thy throne, O God, is for ever and ever;** Here, as in the previous verse, the scripture is introduced as the direct speech of God the Father. B. B. Warfield scathingly refers to those who 'translate vilely, "Thy throne is God."' He said, 'It undoubtedly does not make for edification to observe the expedients which have been resorted to by expositors to escape recognizing that these (messianic) Psalms do ascribe a superhuman nature and superhuman powers to the Messiah.' (*Biblical and Theological Studies*, pp. 88–89) '*God*, in the singular, was a name never given to any creature, but is expressive of his Divine nature, and his relation in the Deity, being God the Son.' (Poole) As the king is divine, His kingdom must endure for ever. 'His it was by natural inheritance, as God the Son; and as man united to the Godhead, he inheriteth the privileges of that person. This natural dominion over all things remaineth for ever.' (Poole) [*Col* 1:16]

**a sceptre of righteousness is the sceptre of thy kingdom.** This expression 'is literally "a sceptre of straightness;" i.e., according to a Hebrew idiom, a straight sceptre. A crooked sceptre was an emblem of an unjust government; a straight sceptre, of a righteous government. The meaning of the poetical description, in plain terms, is – "The administration of Thy kingdom is strictly and invariably just."' (John Brown)

**Thou hast loved righteousness, and hated iniquity;** During the period of his humiliation Christ proved his undeviating attachment to righteousness and his inflexible hatred of iniquity, 'wherefore God also hath highly exalted him, and given him a name which is above every name.' [*Phil* 2:9]

**therefore God, even thy God, hath anointed thee with the oil of gladness** This is a description of the heavenly coronation which followed the victorious completion of Christ's earthly ministry. It is to this event that Peter alludes when he told the Jews on the day of Pentecost 'that God hath made that same Jesus, whom ye have crucified, both Lord and Christ.' [*Acts* 2:36] The unalloyed joy of this occasion distinguishes it from that unction of the Spirit which Christ received when 'he was a man of sorrows, acquainted with grief, and exposed to innumerable evils and troubles.' (John Owen)

**above thy fellows.** 'The angels cannot be intended; their inferiority to the Son is so insisted on here that they could scarcely be described as His "fellows". It is most likely that the reference is to the "many sons" of *ch.* 2:10, whom the firstborn Son is not ashamed to call His "brethren" (*ch.* 2:11) ... Their joy is great, because of their companionship with Him, but His is greater still.' (F. F. Bruce)

*V*10: **And, Thou, Lord, in the beginning hast laid the foundation of the earth; and the heavens are the works of thine hands:**

*V*11: **They shall perish; but thou remainest; and they all shall wax old as doth a garment;**

*V*12: **And as a vesture shalt thou fold them up, and they shall be changed: but thou art the same, and thy years shall not fail.**

The same argument is continued in this quotation of *Psalm* 102:25–27 LXX, from which it is shown that the relation which the angels sustain to Christ is that of creatures to the Creator. This work of creation obviously cannot be ascribed to Christ as man, yet it is here properly assigned to Him as the Eternal Son who became incarnate for our salvation. [cf. *John* 1:3; *Col* 1:16] In verse 12 the Son is further identified as the author of that cataclysmic judgment which finally shall usher in 'new heavens and a new earth, wherein dwelleth righteousness.' [2 *Pet* 3:13] Despite the apparent fixity of the created order the Word of God declares that the cosmos must suffer change, but Christ continues forever in the glorious unity of his theanthropic person. [*Heb* 13:8] This should teach us that 'such is the frailty of the nature of man, and such the perishing condition of all created things, that none can ever obtain the least stable consolation but what ariseth from an interest in the omnipotency, sovereignty, and eternity of the Lord Christ.' (John Owen)

> *Swift to its close ebbs out life's little day;*
> *Earth's joys grow dim, its glories pass away;*
> *Change and decay in all around I see:*
> *O thou who changest not, abide with me.*

*V*13: **But to which of the angels said he at any time, Sit on my right hand, until I make thine enemies thy footstool?**

The rhetorical question which introduces the final quotation from *Psalm* 110:1 demands a negative reply. God never addressed any angel in such terms, but the author plainly infers that He did so speak to the Son. This psalm is cited more frequently in the New Testament than any other, and it is also the foundation upon which the whole superstructure of the Epistle is built. It is the repeated application of the fourth verse of the psalm to Christ which gives the letter its distinctive character, for it shows that He exercises this universal dominion as the enthroned Priest-King, thus combining in His own person two offices which were always kept separate in Israel. In verse one, David hails the Messiah as his Lord because only One who was Himself divine could be advanced by Jehovah to the place of supreme power. 'As he was God, he was David's Lord, but not his son; as he was man, he was David's son, and so absolutely could not be his Lord; in his person, as he was God and man, he was his Lord and his son, – which is the intention of our Saviour's question, *Matt* 22: 45.' (John Owen)

**until I make thine enemies thy footstool?** 'The image is from conquerors putting the feet on the necks of the conquered [*Josh* 10:24, 25].' (A. R. Fausset). Although the word 'until' does not indicate a time when Christ shall cease to reign, 1 *Cor* 15:24 does refer to the end of Christ's mediatorial rule. This passage is explained by Charles Hodge, 'When that is done, i.e., when he has subdued all his enemies, then he will no longer reign over the universe as Mediator, but only as God; while his headship over his people is to continue for ever.' (*Commentary on I Corinthians*, p. 330) As the Church is still constantly attacked by the enemies of Christ it is worth recalling Calvin's seasonable remarks on this verse. 'Certainly if we are to believe what our eyes see, then the kingdom of Christ seems to be on the verge of ruin. But this promise that Christ will never be dragged from His throne but that rather He will lay low all His enemies, banishes from us all fear.'

*V*.14: **Are they not all ministering spirits, sent forth to minister for them who shall be heirs of salvation?**

This question, which requires an affirmative response, places the subordination of the angels in strong contrast with the previous declaration of the Son's sovereignty. As their name implies they are God's messengers 'sent forth to do service for the sake of them that shall inherit salvation.' (RV) This refers to the future possession of the heavenly inheritance. Salvation is a present reality of Christian experience, but its full realization awaits the final consummation. Those who receive salvation as an inheritance clearly have contributed nothing towards it, and this divine patrimony is bestowed upon none but sons. [*John* 1:12, 13] 'Angels' ministrations are not properly *to* men, since the latter cannot command them, though their ministrations *to God* are often *for the good of men*. So the superiority of the Son of God to angels is shown.' (A. R. Fausset)

[27]

# CHAPTER TWO

*V1*: **Therefore we ought to give the more earnest heed to the things which we have heard, lest at any time we should let them slip.**

The author here interjects the first of the warnings with which his argument is punctuated. 'Therefore,' as Christ is so sublimely exalted above the angels, both in His person and His station, how urgent was the need for these Hebrews to give diligent attention to the message of salvation which had been brought to them through Him. This appeal to the glory of Christ lays the axe to the root of the tree of indifference, for a careless hearing of the gospel always stems from a failure to apprehend the unique majesty of the Mediator. [*Matt* 17:5] It was this spiritual lassitude which had exposed them to the very real danger of drifting away from their desired haven.

*V2*: **For if the word spoken by angels was stedfast, and every transgression and disobedience received a just recompence of reward;**

Since there was a strict enforcement of the sanctions denounced against the transgressors of 'the word spoken through angels' (RV), then clearly those who neglect the salvation 'which at the first began to be spoken by the Lord' (*v* 3) will be punished with even greater severity. This argument ex-

pressly contradicts the notion that despisers of the gospel will
be treated with greater leniency than those who disobeyed the
law of Moses. [*Matt* 11:20–24] (On the angelic mediation of
the law see *Acts* 7:53 and *Gal* 3:19.)

*V3*: **How shall we escape, if we neglect so great salvation; which at the first began to be spoken by the Lord,
and was confirmed unto us by them that heard him;**

**How shall we escape,** This serious warning is intended to
dissuade the readers from their contemplated apostasy. The
danger threatened is not imaginary but real. In the previous
verse he reminded them that the penalty inflicted upon the
violators of the law was commensurate with their offence, and
here the emphatic 'we' implies that a far heavier judgment
awaits the despisers of the gospel. [*Heb* 10:29]

**if we neglect** This is tantamount to a deliberate rejection of
it. 'Can any man perish more justly than they who refuse to be
saved?' (John Owen)

**so great** The greatness of this salvation is beyond our com-
putation and our comprehension. [*John* 3:16]

**salvation** The proper end in the publishing of the gospel is
the salvation of those to whom it is sent; the incidental result
is the damnation of those who spurn it. [*Mark* 16:16; *John* 12:
48; *2 Cor* 2:15, 16]

**which at the first began to be spoken by the Lord,** The
finality of the message is indicated by the supreme dignity of
the Messenger through whom it was first proclaimed. [*Matt*
21:37; *Mark* 1:14; *Luke* 4:21; *Heb* 1:2, 3:1]

**and was confirmed unto us by them that heard him;** The
author, 'while distinguishing himself from the apostolic circle,

[29]

everywhere speaks as qualified to set forth a true and authoritative expression of the pre-eminent revelation of the new covenant, a revelation "in a Son" and "spoken through the Lord," and "confirmed unto us by those who heard."' (N. B. Stonehouse, *The Infallible Word*, p. 121)

*V*4: **God also bearing them witness, both with signs and wonders, and with divers miracles, and gifts of the Holy Ghost, according to his own will?**

**God also bearing witness with them,** (RV) This confident appeal to the miraculous display of divine power which accompanied the apostolic proclamation of the gospel obviously could never have been made if the wonders here described were completely unknown to the recipients of this Epistle. But it is equally unreasonable to expect the continuous manifestation of similar supernatural signs when there is now no new gospel to confirm and the canon of Scripture is complete. These gifts 'were part of the credentials of the Apostles as the authoritative agents of God in founding the church. Their function thus confined them to distinctively the Apostolic Church, and they necessarily passed away with it.' (B. B. Warfield on 'The Cessation of the Charismata,' in *Miracles: Yesterday and Today, Real and Counterfeit*, p. 6)

**both by signs and wonders, and by manifold powers,** (RV) '"Signs" (SĒMEIA) are miracles, or other facts regarded as *proofs* of a divine mission; "wonders" (TERATA) are miracles viewed as prodigies, causing *astonishment* [*Acts* 2:22, 23]; "powers" (DUNAMEIS) are miracles viewed as manifestations of superhuman *power*.' (A. R. Fausset)

**and by gifts of the Holy Ghost, according to his own will?** (RV) 'The Holy Ghost, being the Spirit of God, is bestowed according to the will of God, and, though one, He is given in such a way to men that they appear with very dissimilar spiritual endowments (1 *Cor* 12:4, 11]; and the signal spiritual gifts attending the apostolic preaching both showed that God was most present with it, and marked it as the opening of the new dispensation [*Joel* 2:28] and the inbreaking of the world to come [*Heb* 6:5].' (A. B. Davidson)

*V5*: **For unto the angels hath he not put in subjection the world to come, whereof we speak.**

These Hebrews had become discouraged partly because they did not as yet possess those external blessings which they associated with the world to come. Their preoccupation with the future had made them blind to their present spiritual privileges, a disease which the author seeks to cure by insisting upon the reality of Christ's present rule. The old world was placed in subjection to the angels when sin broke man's dominion over it, but the new world began with the heavenly enthronement of Christ as the victorious Son of Man. Christianity 'thus marks the beginning of the future world. The author speaks of the great salvation of Christianity, which is so great because God has subjected the inhabited world to the rule of His people. This was the original goal of creation, but it was effected only in Christ. With Christ, therefore, we have a new creation.' (G. Vos)

*V6*: **But one in a certain place testified, saying, What is man, that thou art mindful of him? or the son of man, that thou visitest him?**

*V7*: **Thou madest him a little lower than the angels; thou crownedst him with glory and honour, and didst set him over the works of thy hands:**

*V8a*: **Thou hast put all things in subjection under his feet.**

In confirmation of his contention the author reminds his readers of a passage of Scripture which is well known to them. [Ps 8:4–6] The Psalmist is filled with awe as he contemplates the works of God, and he marvels at the Creator's mercy towards frail and fallen man. For sin made man mortal, and by this punishment God reduced 'him "below the angels" in a point in which he once was on a level with them.' (John Brown) Nevertheless this period of subjection to the angels is to be superseded by man's final exaltation over them. 'As no limitation occurs in the Scripture, the "all things" must include heavenly, as well as earthly things.' (A. R. Fausset) [1 Cor 6:3] Thus the terms of this prediction are such that it could find fulfilment only in 'the man Christ Jesus,' to whom it is immediately applied. (v 9)

*V*8b: **For in that he put all in subjection under him, he left nothing that is not put under him. But now we see not yet all things put under him.**

This oracle therefore means that God has excepted nothing from the sovereignty of man, but present experience sadly proves that the full accomplishment of this divine decree is still awaited.

*V*9: **But we see Jesus, who was made a little lower than the angels by the suffering of death, crowned with glory and honour; that he by the grace of God should taste death for every man.** (AV margin)

However, the application of the prophecy to Jesus exhibits the certainty of its realization, for faith perceives that the final glorification of the members is guaranteed by the present exaltation of the Head. But Jesus is now 'crowned with glory and honour' because he first consented to be 'made a little lower than the angels.' 'In becoming man Christ took upon Him a nature that was *capable* of dying. This the angels were not; and in *this* respect He was, for a season, made lower than they.' (Arthur Pink) Furthermore his death was no peaceful quietus for he willingly came to drain to its bitterest dregs the cup which our sins had mingled. (James Denney)

**that** The word expresses purpose and introduces the clause which explains the reason for Christ's death.

**he by the grace of God** 'This intimates that unmerited grace prompted God to give His Son, and to transfer guilt to Him. In short, whatever was vicarious was of grace in a special sense. A penal death was the effect of justice; but to admit a Surety-substitution was of grace.' (G. Smeaton)

**should taste death** 'So that Christ by tasting of death had experience, knew what was in death, as threatened unto sinners. He found out and understood what bitterness was in that cup wherein it was given him.' (John Owen)

**for every man.** The scope of this declaration is determined by the context, which shows that Christ died for 'the heirs of salvation' [1:14], the 'many sons' [2:10], those who are 'sanctified' [2:11], his 'brethren' [2:11, 12], and the 'children' whom God had given him [2:13]. 'Christ did taste death for every son to be brought to glory and for all the children whom God had given to him. But there is not the slightest warrant in this text to extend the reference of the vicarious death of Christ beyond those who are most expressly referred to in the context. This text shows how plausible off-hand quotation may be and yet how baseless is such an appeal in support of a doctrine of universal atonement.' (John Murray, *Redemption Accomplished and Applied*, p. 61)

*V*10: **For it became him, for whom are all things, and by whom are all things, in bringing many sons unto glory, to make the captain of their salvation perfect through sufferings.**

Although man idly dreams of salvation without atonement, this is a forcible reminder that it can never be safe to dispense with what is deemed to be necessary by Him who is the Creator of all things and the sovereign Disposer of all events. The readers of the Epistle must resist the temptation to renounce their faith in a crucified Messiah because the glorification of the 'many sons' could only be secured through the humiliation of their redeeming Head, who thus became the 'author' (RV) of their salvation. As Geerhardus Vos points out, the word 'perfect' does not mean that 'Christ stood in need of *moral* improvement.' It rather indicates that His endurance of these sufferings perfectly fitted Him to exercise this office for His people. 'Such is the desert of sin, and such is the immutability of the justice of God, that there was no way possible to bring sinners unto glory but by the death and sufferings of the Son of God, who undertook to be the captain of their salvation.' (John Owen)

*V*II: **For both he that sanctifieth and they who are sanctified are all of one: for which cause he is not ashamed to call them brethren,**

The character of this salvation is further defined by this description of the work which Christ performs for His people. He is the author of their sanctification. This does not here refer to a continuous process; it means that Christ has cleansed His people from their sin in order to make them fit to serve God. 'Purifying, sanctifying, perfecting, lie with Paul in the moral subjective sphere, as is especially clear in the case of "sanctification." But in Hebrews the last named has as a rule nothing to do with the subjective moral transformation of the believer. It describes, on the contrary, what has been done through the sacrifice of Jesus outside of the believer, to render the way to God open for him. In Pauline language we should call this "justification," although that would not exactly reproduce the point of view.' (G. Vos, *The Self-Disclosure of Jesus*, p. 301) It is because the sanctifier and the sanctified are partakers of the same nature that 'he is not ashamed to call them brethren.' Arthur Pink points out that if 'all of one' alluded to God as their common father this denial of shame would have been entirely out of place, for 'he could not then do otherwise than call them brethren.' The whole passage is intended to bring 'out the oneness of Christ with His people in their humiliation. In other words, the apostle is not here speaking of our being lifted up to Christ's level, but of His coming down to ours.' John Owen is at pains to show the inconsistency of those who have no desire to own Christ as their sanctifier and yet wish to claim him as the 'captain of their salvation.' 'There is surely, then, a woeful mistake in the world. If Christ sanctifies all whom he saves, many will appear to have been mistaken in their expectations another day.'

*V*12: **Saying, I will declare thy name unto my brethren, in the midst of the church will I sing praise unto thee.**

Three testimonies are next introduced to prove that Christ is the Head of a new order of humanity, the first of which is from *Psalm* 22:22. This is taken from that part of the psalm which predicts the triumphant sequel to the Messiah's sufferings. [*John* 20:17] 'The constitution of the "congregation" or *church*, with Christ in the midst revealing God to His brethren, is possible only because of His sacrifice.' (A. M. Stibbs)

*V*13: **And again, I will put my trust in him. And again, Behold I and the children which God hath given me.**

It is because the national rejection of the Messiah was uniquely foreshadowed by Isaiah's own experience that his words are here fitly applied to Christ. [*Is* 8:17 LXX, 8:18) Although his faithfulness to the divine commission had separated him from the nation at large the prophet continued to trust in God.

However this isolation was not complete, for his ministry also resulted in the emergence of an elect remnant, even 'the children which God hath given me.' [cf. *Is* 6:13] 'This identification extended not only to his disciples, of whom we read, but also to his children. These children were given him precisely for the express purpose of being identified with him in his trust in God. They were children of prophetic significance. Centuries later this was repeated, on a higher plane, in Christ. Again there was an unparalleled necessity for Christ to put his trust in God, and also there arose a close identification between Christ and the believers.' (G. Vos) This passage, which is unique in describing believers as the children of Christ, strongly emphasizes His humanity. For Christ could not save the children whom God had given Him in the eternal covenant of grace without first becoming their Kinsman-Redeemer, and He could not put his trust in God except as he was made the Son of Man. [*John* 17:2]

*V*14: **Forasmuch then as the children are partakers of flesh and blood, he also himself likewise took part of the same; that through death he might destroy him that had the power of death, that is, the devil;**

**Since then the children are sharers in flesh and blood, he also himself in like manner partook of the same;** (RV) 'Flesh and blood' was foreign to his existence as the Eternal Son of God, but Christ willingly 'partook of the same' in order to secure the salvation of His children. In thus stating the purpose of the incarnation, the author also removes its stigma, for as John Owen rightly insists, 'the first and principal end of the Lord Christ's assuming human nature, was not to reign in it, but to suffer and die in it.'

**that through death he might bring to nought him that had the power of death, that is, the devil;** (RV) The children of Christ could only be delivered from the devil's dominion by His dying the death which was properly theirs. It was His vicarious endurance of the penalty of sin which annulled death's condemning power over them and made it but the portal to eternal life. [1 *Cor* 15:55-57] 'Jesus suffering death overcame: Satan wielding death succumbed.' (Bengel, cited by A. R. Fausset)

## *V*15: **And deliver them who through fear of death were all their lifetime subject to bondage.**

'The judgment of God always shows itself in consciousness of sin. It is from this fear that Christ has released us, by undergoing our curse, and thus taking away what was fearful in death. Although we must still meet death, let us nevertheless be calm and serene in living and dying, when we have Christ going before us. If anyone cannot set his mind at rest by disregarding death, that man should know that he has not yet gone far enough in the faith of Christ.' (Calvin) [*Heb* 9:27] Scripture proclaims freedom from the fear of death through the finished work of Christ, but the best that atheistic philosophy can recommend to modern man is the free acceptance of death as the natural termination of his existence. Those who choose to experience such an authentic 'existence,' thereby deprive themselves of that 'life' more abundant which is found only in the living Lord Himself. [*Rev* 1:18][1]

## *V*16: **For verily he taketh not hold of angels, but of the seed of Abraham he taketh hold.** (AV margin)

The Son became man because God designed to save men, and not the angels who lost their first estate. The same verb is used in *Hebrews* 8:9 graphically to depict God's deliverance of His

[1] For a critical evaluation of Existentialism the interested reader is referred to J. M. Spier's *Christianity and Existentialism*.

people from their bondage in Egypt. 'He assumed into union with his person the seed of Abraham; which seed is not to be understood here collectively, for either his carnal or believing seed; but it is the one singular, eminent Seed of Abraham, in and by whom, himself, his seed, and all nations were to be blessed, *Gen* 22:18, compare *Gal* 3:16, the man Christ Jesus.' (Poole) John Owen makes the succinct comment, 'Here sovereign grace interposeth, – the love of God to mankind, *Tit* 3:4. As to the angels, he "spared them not," 2 *Pet* 2:4. He spared not them, and "spared not his Son" for us, *Rom* 8:32.'

**V17: Wherefore in all things it behoved him to be made like unto his brethren, that he might be a merciful and faithful high priest in things pertaining to God, to make reconciliation for the sins of the people.**

This conformity of Christ to His brethren in 'all things,' sin only excepted [cf. *Heb* 4:15], was necessary so that He might become their High Priest and thus 'make propitiation for the sins of the people.' (RV) [*Heb* 5:1, 2] 'As the Jewish high priest brought the atonement for the people of the old economy once every year, so Christ, once for all, satisfied divine justice, and removed the penalty of sin by His historic oblation at Jerusalem as Priest and Sacrifice in one person. The term PROPITIATE means to appease God, or to avert His wrath by sacrifice; and the passage is not to be interpreted of intercession in heaven, though that follows and leans on the sacrifice, but of the one propitiation or atonement of the cross.' (G. Smeaton) The word 'propitiate' appears here with sin as the object, and as it is obviously impossible to propitiate sin, it has been urged with some cogency that the word 'expiation' should be adopted instead. But as F. F. Bruce remarks, 'if sins require to be expiated, it is beause they are sins committed against someone who ought to be propitiated.' Christ therefore made propitiation in respect of the sins of His people, and it is by this satisfaction of divine justice that He gained access to God on their behalf.[1] As the Jews did not expect a suffering Messiah, the Cross was the great stumbling block to their faith in Him, but this explanation of the purpose of Christ's humiliation is sufficient to demonstrate its necessity.

*V*18: **For in that he himself hath suffered being tempted, he is able to succour them that are tempted.**

Christ's triumph over the temptations which arose out of His sufferings, gave Him the perpetual ability to aid 'them that are tempted.' For, as Thomas Hewitt so finely says, 'the power of sympathy does not depend on the experience of sin, but on the experience of the strength of the temptation to sin which only the sinless can know in its full intensity.'

[1] Further information on this important subject is given in the articles on 'Expiation' and 'Propitiation' by Leon Morris in *The New Bible Dictionary*.

# CHAPTER THREE

In this chapter the author approaches the problem of proving Christ's superiority to Moses with great finesse, as any criticism of their renowned Leader and Lawgiver would only antagonize his readers and prevent all further discussion. In fact this point was conceded in principle when he established the Son's ascendancy over the angels, for even the Jews did not regard Moses as being equal to them. However, it will be seen that in exalting Christ he does not find it necessary to defame Moses.

*V*1: **Wherefore, holy brethren, partakers of the heavenly calling, consider the Apostle and High Priest of our profession, Christ Jesus;**

**Wherefore,** 'i.e., Seeing we have such a sympathizing Helper, you ought to "contemplate attentively," fix your mind on Him, so as to profit by the contemplation (*ch* 12:2).' (A. R. Fausset)

**holy brethren,** These Hebrews are reminded that their confession of faith in Christ at once made them members of a holy brotherhood and separated them from their unbelieving kinsmen. [*Heb* 2:11]

**partakers of the heavenly calling,** The earthly rest of Canaan only faintly reflected the reality of the heavenly inheritance which Christ calls His people to share. 'In the word "heavenly" there is struck for the first time, in words at least, an antithesis of great importance in the Epistle, that of this world and heaven, in other words that of the merely material and transient and the ideal and abiding. The things of this world are material, unreal, transient; those of heaven are ideal, true, and eternal.' (A. B. Davidson)

**consider** The word means 'notice in a spiritual sense, fix the eyes of the spirit upon someone.' (Arndt-Gingrich) If the author 'could but get the Hebrew Christians to *"consider* the Apostle and High Priest of their profession,"* his object of keeping them steady in their attachment to Him was gained. It is because men do not know Christ that they do not love Him; it is because they know Him so imperfectly that they love Him so imperfectly. The truth about Him as the Great Prophet and the Great High Priest well deserves consideration – it is "the manifold wisdom of God." It requires it; it cannot be understood by a careless, occasional glance.' (John Brown)

**the Apostle and High Priest** The prophetic and priestly functions of Christ are here closely conjoined by the single definite article. (G. Vos) The writer avoids giving the title 'apostle' to the first preachers of the gospel in *ch* 2:4 because he chooses to reserve it for the One whom God has sent into the world and through whom God is supremely revealed to man. [*Heb* 1:1, 2] 'As Prophet, Christ is God's representative to His people; as Priest, He is their representative before God. As the Apostle He speaks *to* us from God, as our High Priest He speaks *for* us to God.' (Arthur Pink)

**of our confession, even Jesus;** (RV) The word 'our' is said by John Owen to be 'added by way of discrimination' and means, – 'Whatever by others he be esteemed, he is so to us; and our inestimable privilege and honour it is that he is so.'

*V*2: **Who was faithful to him that appointed him, as also Moses was faithful in all his house.**

The verse disarms prejudice by according Moses the highest praise. In the household of God, Moses resembles Jesus in his faithfulness, for though he was not without personal failings, his ministerial fidelity was beyond question. 'He withheld nothing of what God revealed or commanded, nor did he add any thing thereunto; and herein did his faithfulness consist.' (John Owen) [*Num* 12:7] But the faithfulness of Moses could be exercised only during the limited period of his earthly service, whereas Jesus ever lives faithfully to exercise the office of Divine Mediator from His throne in heaven. (ONTA '*being faithful*'). [*Acts* 2:36; *Heb* 5:5].

*V*3: **For this man was counted worthy of more glory than Moses, inasmuch as he who hath builded the house hath more honour than the house.**

Since Christ is the builder of this household, His glory far excels that of Moses who was but a servant in it and a member of it. Christ is worthy of their worship for the supernatural work which has been entrusted to Him by God demands nothing less than divinity for its accomplishment. But every form of worship which is directed to God through a mere creature is idolatry. 'To give this honour unto saints, angels, or others, is men's invention, not God's institution. God knows how to give glory unto his servants without imparting unto them his own, the royalty of his crown: "his glory will he not give unto another."'(John Owen)

*V*4: **For every house is builded by some man; but he that built all things is God.**

'Some one must be the founder of every house: Moses was not the founder, but a portion of the house (but He who established all things, *and therefore* the spiritual house, is God). Christ, being instrumentally the Founder of all things, must be the Founder of the house, so greater than Moses.' (A. R. Fausset) [*Heb* 1:2]

***V5***: **And Moses verily was faithful in all his house, as a servant, for a testimony of those things which were to be spoken after;**

Instead of calling Moses a bondservant, the writer uses another word which draws attention to the unique dignity of his station in all 'God's house.' (RV margin) [cf. *Num* 12:7 LXX] However, there was no finality in the institutions and testimonies he delivered to Israel for these all pointed forward to the promised Messiah. [*Luke* 24:27; *John* 5:46; *Heb* 10:1] Moreover he plainly acknowledged the preparatory character of the revelation which was mediated through him when he predicted the advent of another Prophet whom God would raise up from among them. [*Deut* 18:15, 18–19] 'And here the apostle takes his leave of Moses, – he treats not about him any more; and therefore he gives him as it were an honourable burial. He puts this glorious epitaph on his grave, "Moses, a faithful servant of the Lord in his whole house."'(John Owen)

***V6***: **But Christ as a son over his own house; whose house are we, if we hold fast the confidence and the rejoicing of the hope firm unto the end.**

**But Christ as a son over his own house;** Moses and Christ are both said to be faithful, but even in this there is similarity and not identity, for faithfulness is to be gauged by the sphere in which it is exercised. The faithfulness of Moses was finite and temporal, but that of Christ is infinite and eternal. Moses was *within* the house as a faithful *servant*; Christ faithfully presided *over* the same house as the Messianic *Son*. In Christ there is therefore a radical spiritual continuity between the period of promise and the age of fulfilment. [1 *Cor* 10:4; *Heb* 11:26]

**whose house are we, if we hold fast the confidence and the rejoicing of the hope firm unto the end.** Their profession of faith in Christ had marked them out as members of this household, but they must be careful to maintain their personal confidence in the Christian hope. [*Rom* 5:2] Christians do not entertain a delusive confidence, and this is solely because Christ is the substance of their hope. Those who fail to continue 'firm unto the end' do not overthrow the doctrine of the final perseverance of the saints; they simply prove that they were never really a part of Christ's house. 'The Hebrews were ever in danger of subordinating the future to the present, and of forsaking the invisible (Christ in heaven) for the visible (Judaism on earth), of giving up a profession which involved them in fierce persecution. Hence their need of being reminded that the proof of *their* belonging to the house of Christ was that they remained steadfast to Him to the end of their pilgrimage.' (Arthur Pink)

*V*7: **Wherefore (as the Holy Ghost saith, To day if ye will hear his voice,**

As the AV correctly indicates, the parenthetical quotation of *Psalm* 95. 7–11 is introduced to enforce the exhortation 'Wherefore . . . take heed.' (*v* 12) The relevance of this testimony to the crisis of decision which now faced them is strikingly conveyed in the words 'as the Holy Ghost saith.' In describing this psalm as the authoritative utterance of the Holy Spirit the writer not only points to its inspiration, but he also emphasizes the peril of regarding Scripture as a dead letter, for its Divine Author continues to speak directly to mankind in it. [*Heb* 4: 12] 'To-day' refers to that period of grace which God grants to men. Those who fall short of the promised inheritance do so by their failure to respond to the last of these daily invitations. Thus their disbelief in the Word of God is an act of disobedience which effectively excludes them from entering into

His rest. (*v* 19) God's word is always 'To-day', but it is never safe to presume that He will say it again 'Tomorrow!' [2 *Cor* 6:2] The author is fearful lest his readers should have reached just such a point of no return for he compares their situation with that which faced their fathers in the wilderness.

*V*8: **Harden not your hearts, as in the provocation, in the day of temptation in the wilderness:**

**Harden not your hearts,** 'It is to the *heart* God's word is addressed, that moral centre of our beings out of which are the issues of life [*Prov* 4:23]. There may be conviction of the conscience, the assent of the intellect, the admiration of the understanding, but unless the heart is moved there is no response.' (Arthur Pink)

**as in the provocation, in the day of temptation in the wilderness:** 'Temptation' and 'provocation' refer to the incidents at Massah and Meribah. [*Exod* 17:1–7; *Num* 20:1–13] These examples of Israel's unbelief which occurred at the beginning and the end of their wanderings in the wilderness suggest that the whole of their course was characterized by a progressive hardening of heart.

*V*9: **When your fathers tempted me, proved me, and saw my works forty years.**

**Where your fathers tempted me by proving me,** (RV margin) There in the desert they put God to the test to see if He were worthy of their trust. 'The lesson to the Hebrew Christians is, their "to-day" is to last only between the first preaching of the Gospel and Jerusalem's impending overthrow – viz., FORTY YEARS; exactly the number of years of Israel's sojourn in the wilderness, until, the full measure of guilt having been filled up, all the rebels were overthrown.' (A. R. Fausset)

[45]

*V*10: **Wherefore I was grieved with that generation, and said, They do alway err in their heart; and they have not known my ways.**

'Grieved' is too mild a word, for the Psalmist expressed God's disgust with that generation because 'they do alway err in their heart' and 'they did not know my ways.' (RV) 'Alway' points to the permanent and prevailing bent of their heart. As this condition was habitual their case was hopeless. Moreover, though they were not without a knowledge of God's will for them, they preferred to walk in their own ways, thus proving their complete unfitness to enter into the rest of God.

*V*11: **So I sware in my wrath, They shall not enter into my rest.)**

The disobedience which excluded them from the earthly rest of Canaan also debarred them from sharing in the eternal rest of heaven, 'for God took their faith or unbelief in this proximate sense as having an eternal and final effect.' (G. Vos)

'Old Testament examples are New Testament instructions.' (John Owen) [1 *Cor* 10:11]

*V*12: **Take heed, brethren, lest there be in any of you an evil heart of unbelief, in departing from the living God.**

All are affectionately addressed as 'brethren', but each is warned of the peril he faced, for none could abandon Christ without also 'departing from the living God.' [*Heb* 2:3] It is perfectly safe to depart from the dead gods of the heathen, but it is otherwise with Him who lives to make His threatened punishments an awful reality. [*Heb* 10:31] The faithless heart is here described as evil because the root of all apostasy is the primal sin of unbelief. [*Gen* 3:1]

[46]

*V*13 : **But exhort one another daily, while it is called To day; lest any of you be hardened through the deceitfulness of sin.**

They are urged to improve each day of grace by mutual exhortation in order to escape being hardened by the deceitfulness of sin. Sin first gained its power over mankind by assuming an attractive disguise, but its hideous character is revealed by the Word of God which strips it of this fair façade. It is only when the mask is so pierced that sin loses its power to charm. [*Gen* 3:13; 2 *Cor* 11:3; *Gal* 6:7]

'All the devices of sin are as fair baits whereby dangerous hooks are covered over to entice silly fish to snap at them, so as they are taken and made a prey to the fisher.' (Dr. Gouge, cited by Arthur Pink)

*V*14 : **For we are made partakers of Christ, if we hold the beginning of our confidence stedfast unto the end;**

'We have become sharers of Christ' (Lenski) is a charitable acknowledgment of their profession which must be proved genuine by their patient perseverance to the end. As Kenneth Wuest well says, 'Again as in verse 6, the question is not one of the *retention* of salvation based upon a *persistence* of faith, but of the *possession* of salvation as evidenced by a *continuation* of faith.' This expression should not be understood in the Pauline sense of mystical union with Christ, but it more probably points to their participation in Christ's heavenly kingdom. [*Heb* 12:28]

*V*15 : **While it is said, To day if ye will hear his voice, harden not your hearts, as in the provocation.**

The repetition of the quotation begins a new section which enforces the lesson to be learned from the example of their forefathers. [*vv* 15–19]

**While it is said, To day** The urgency of the appeal is dictated by this limitation of the opportunity to hear God's voice. 'The doors of God's rest are closed to those who obdurately will not obey the voice of grace in the blessed "today" nor heed its warning.' (Lenski)

*V*16: **For some, when they had heard, did provoke: howbeit not all that came out of Egypt by Moses.**

As the verse makes better sense as a question than a statement the RV is preferable here. It is only the placing of an accent which accounts for the difference between 'some' (AV) and 'who' (RV).

**For who, when they heard, did provoke? nay, did not all they that came out of Egypt by Moses?** (RV) 'All who left Egypt did not enter Canaan. All who by profession leave the world lying in wickedness do not, of course, enter into the heavenly rest. Men may hear the Gospel, and yet not believe it. The grace of God may come to them, and yet come to them in vain. But this is not all. The great majority – almost all who came out of Egypt with Moses, almost all who heard the promise and command of God – were unbelieving and disobedient. Was not this a most striking demonstration of the strength of the natural tendency to unbelief and disobedience in the human heart? And was it not reasonable and right that the Hebrews should take heed lest there was in any of them "an evil heart of unbelief," when it was so plain that there was such a heart in the great majority of their ancestors?' (John Brown) [*Num* 26:64, 65]

*V*17: **But with whom was he grieved forty years? was it not with them that had sinned, whose carcases fell in the wilderness?**

The author chose to set forth the consequences of Israel's unbelief in a series of questions because this rhetorical device was
better fitted to touch the consciences of his readers than a
simple statement of the facts. In this verse he traces the inevitable connection between God's displeasure and the ex-
emplary judgment which overtook those who sinned in the
wilderness. [1 Cor 10:5–11] 'Moses and others of God's own
cannot be numbered among these sinners, for their sins were
pardoned and persons accepted; and though they came short
of the literal, had a much more abundant entrance administered
to them into the heavenly Canaan.' (Poole)

V18: **And to whom sware he that they should not enter
into his rest, but to them that believed not?**

**but to them that were disobedient?** (RV) Unbelief is that
form of disobedience which by way of eminence excludes
men from enjoying the rest of God, for as Augustine re-
marked, 'while it continues, all other sins are retained, and
when it departs all other sins are remitted.' (cited by G.
Smeaton, *The Doctrine of the Holy Spirit*, p. 178) [Mark 16:16;
John 16:9]

V19: **So we see that they could not enter in because of
unbelief.**

'Unbelief deprives men of all interest in or right unto the
promises of God. There was a promise given unto this people
of their being brought into the land of Canaan; but yet they
entered not into it, – they died in the wilderness. How came
this to pass? The apostle here declares that they disinherited
themselves, and lost all their interest in the promise, by their
unbelief. And let not others entertain better hopes of their
condition hereafter, whilst here they follow their example;
for, – No unbeliever shall ever enter into the rest of God.'
(John Owen)

# CHAPTER FOUR

*V*1: **Let us therefore fear, lest, a promise being left us of entering into his rest, any of you should seem to come short of it.**

Although the promise of entering into the rest of God still remained open, they had reason to fear lest any one of them should be thought to have fallen short of it after the evil example of their faithless forbears. [*Heb* 3:19] Had such warnings been superfluous they would not have been given. A healthy sense of self-distrust must always accompany faith in the Word of God, for while those elected to eternal life can never be lost, the child of God is actually saved by paying heed to those warnings which are annexed to the divine promise. Those best acquainted with the plague of their own hearts will never deem it safe to dispense with what God considers to be necessary for their spiritual safety. [1 *Cor* 10:12; *Phil* 2:12]

*V*2: **For unto us was the gospel preached, as well as unto them: but the word preached did not profit them, not being mixed with faith in them that heard it.**

The lesson to be learned from the past must not be lost upon the readers, for their fathers in the wilderness also heard the glad tidings of salvation, but 'the word which they heard did not benefit them, because it was not united by faith with the hearers.' (Arndt-Gingrich) [1 *Cor* 10:4] Faith must be commingled with 'the word preached' if it is to profit those who hear it. 'Faith and the promise meeting make a happy mixture, a precious confection.' (John Trapp)

*V*3 : **For we which have believed do enter into rest, as he said, As I have sworn in my wrath, if they shall enter into my rest: although the works were finished from the foundation of the world.**

*V*4 : **For he spake in a certain place of the seventh day on this wise, And God did rest the seventh day from all his works.**

*V*5 : **And in this place again, If they shall enter into my rest.**

It should be noted that the av somewhat misleadingly gives a literal translation of the Greek in verses 3 and 5, 'if they shall enter into my rest', which in fact means 'they shall not enter into my rest.' (rv) And this further citation of *Psalm* 95:11 (cf. 3:11) is introduced to show that if the divine oath excludes all unbelievers from a share in that rest into which God entered when He finished the work of creation, then it also follows that the invitation to participate in this rest remains open for all believers. 'Wherever there is a promise, there a threatening in reference unto the same matter is tacitly understood. And wherever there is a threatening, that is no more than so, be it never so severe, there is a gracious promise included in it; yea, sometimes God gives out an express threatening for no other end but that men may lay hold on the promise tacitly included. The threatening that Nineveh should perish was given out that it might not perish. And John Baptist's preaching that the axe was laid to the root of the trees was a call to repent-

ance, that none might be cut down and cast into the fire.'
(John Owen)

The repetition of the divine sentence pronounced on Israel
in verse 5 *after* the testimony which confirmed that God's rest
was available to man since the completion of the work of
creation is a solemn reminder that this rest will never be attained by the disobedient. [*Gen* 2:2; *Exod* 20:11, 31:17; *Ps*
95:11]

'God did rest the seventh day – a rest not ending with the
seventh day, but beginning then, and still continuing, into
which believers enter. God's rest is not a rest necessitated by
fatigue, nor consisting in idleness, but that upholding and
governing of which creation was the beginning. (*Alford*)
Hence Moses records the end of each of the first six days, but
not of the seventh.' (A. R. Fausset) Now God established the
pattern upon which man's life was to be built by following
the cycle of His creative activity with this 'day' of rest.

In Hebrew thought the word 'rest' has a positive meaning
and 'stands for consummation of a work accomplished and
the joy and satisfaction attendant upon this. Such was its
prototype in God. . . . For mankind, too, a great task awaits
to be accomplished, and at its close beckons a rest of joy and
satisfaction that shall copy the rest of God. Before all other
important things, therefore, the Sabbath is an expression of
the eschatological principle on which the life of humanity has
been constructed. . . . It teaches its lesson through the rhyth-
mical succession of six days of labour and one ensuing day of
rest in each successive week. Man is reminded in this way that
life is not an aimless existence, that a goal lies beyond.' (G.
Vos, *Biblical Theology*, pp. 156–157)

*V*6: **Seeing therefore it remaineth that some must enter
therein, and they to whom it was first preached entered
not in because of unbelief:**

In summing up the preceding verses (3–5), the author concludes that it is God's desire that men should enter into His rest, and that this gracious design cannot be frustrated by the disobedience of those to whom this good news was first preached. The refusals of unbelief can never nullify the promise of an entrance into God's rest, for others will be bidden to take their place. [*Matt* 22:8–10; *Acts* 13:46]

*V*7: **Again, he limiteth a certain day, saying in David, To day, after so long a time; as it is said, To day if ye will hear his voice, harden not your hearts.**

It makes no material difference whether the author regarded the 95th Psalm as a composition of David's (as in the LXX) or whether 'saying in David' simply means 'in the book of David.' What matters is that God is still speaking this word of warning and invitation to these wavering Hebrews through the testimony of 'David.' And if they should choose to ignore these repeated admonitions they have no reason to expect that they will fare any better than those who perished in the wilderness for exactly the same fault.

*V*8: **For if Joshua had given them rest, then would he not afterward have spoken of another day.** (AV margin)

Moreover, if this rest had been enjoyed by those who eventually possessed Canaan under the leadership of Joshua, then God would not have fixed another day for entering into it so long afterwards. (*v* 7) For the temporal settlement of the promised land was but a faint shadow of the true rest into which the people of God are conducted by their 'Joshua' who is, as Trapp says, 'Jehovah our Righteousness.' [*Matt* 11:28–30]

*V*9: **There remaineth therefore a rest to the people of God.**

**There remaineth therefore a sabbath rest for the people of God.** (RV) The word SABBATISMOS occurs only here in the New Testament and it means 'keeping of a Sabbath.' (AV margin) As those addressed might feel that their faith in Christ had deprived them of a Sabbath rest, the author seeks to allay these fears by showing that Christ's work invested it with a new significance. The Sabbath was a creation ordinance which placed the day of rest at the end of the six days of labour, but when Adam sinned it became impossible for man to attain the rest of God by his own efforts. This now required nothing less than a second creation, and by keeping the Sabbath on the first day of the week, 'the people of God' gladly acknowledge that their entrance into this rest depends entirely upon the redemptive achievement of Christ. 'Believers knew themselves in a measure partakers of the Sabbath-fulfilment. If the one creation required one sequence, then the other required another. It has been strikingly observed, that our Lord died on the eve of that Jewish Sabbath, at the end of one of these typical weeks of labour by which His work and its consummation were prefigured. And Christ entered upon His rest, the rest of His new, eternal life on the first day of the week, so that the Jewish Sabbath comes to lie between, was as it were, disposed of, buried in His grave. (Delitzsch)' (G. Vos, *Biblical Theology*, p. 158)

*V*10: **For he that is entered into his rest, he also hath ceased from his own works, as God did from his.**

John Brown correctly maintains that this rest may not be restricted to the future state of 'celestial blessedness' but that it pertains to the believer's present condition. Accordingly, he understands this verse to mean: 'He who has entered into his rest has fellowship with God – rests along with God; and therefore the rest well deserves to be called a sabbatism – a sacred rest. He who believes the truth enters on the enjoyment of a happiness which is of the same nature, and springs from the same sources, as the happiness of God. Jehovah rests and rejoices in the manifestation made of His all-perfect character in the person and work of Jesus Christ; and he who believes enters into this rest, and participates of this joy.'

*V11*: **Let us labour therefore to enter into that rest, lest any man fall after the same example of unbelief.**

The urgency of this exhortation stems from the very real danger of falling short of God's rest. Once again the allusion is to those whose carcasses 'fell' in the wilderness, and here the verb points to the complete ruin of any one who follows 'the same example of disobedience.' (RV) [*Num* 14:29; *Heb* 3:17] For as Trapp remarks, 'God hangs up some malefactors, as it were in gibbets, for a warning to others.' In order to avoid this unhappy fate it is vital that they spare no pains and make every effort to enter into that rest which is offered to them in the gospel.

*V12*: **For the word of God is quick, and powerful, and sharper than any twoedged sword, piercing even to the dividing asunder of soul and spirit, and of the joints and marrow, and is a discerner of the thoughts and intents of the heart.**

In case anyone might be tempted to treat God's Word as a 'dead' letter which could be ignored with impunity, the admonition is reinforced by the stern reminder that it is 'living and active' (RV) and so is quick to detect and punish the first secret stirrings of unbelief in the heart. The context makes it certain that the phrase 'sharper than any twoedged sword' has no reference to the activity of the divine Word in regeneration but rather describes its terrible power to execute the sentence which it passes upon rebels who resist its testimony. 'The qualities attributed to *the word of God* show that it is regarded in its JUDICIAL power, whereby it doomed the disobedient Israelites to exclusion from Canaan, and shall exclude unbelieving Christians from the heavenly rest.' (A. R. Fausset) On the expression – 'piercing even to the dividing of soul and spirit, of both joints and marrow' – F. F. Bruce remarks, 'It would indeed be precarious to draw any conclusions from these words about our author's psychology, nor is it necessary to understand them in the sense of the Pauline distinction between soul and spirit.'[1]

*V*13: **Neither is there any creature that is not manifest in his sight: but all things are naked and opened unto the eyes of him with whom we have to do.**

Since 'everything is open and laid bare to the eyes' (Arndt-Gingrich) of Him to whom we must give account, how important it is for us to strive earnestly to enter into His rest. 'In the wrestler's art TRACHĒLISMOS was a grip of the antagonist's throat akin to the bandit's *garotte*, rendering him limp and powerless . . . This characteristic figure then may be held to represent either the denuded or helpless plight of all created persons or forces when brought face to face with their Creator and Lord.' (E. K. Simpson, cited by F. F. Bruce) Hence Calvin wisely concludes, 'Whenever His Word is set before us, we must tremble, because nothing is hid from Him.'

---

[1] J. G. Machen regards the threefold division of man's nature into body, soul, and spirit as a serious error because it encourages what he calls 'an "empty-room" view of the presence of God in the redeemed man.' It suggests that only the 'spiritual' part of man requires renovation, whereas Scripture teaches 'that the whole man, corrupt before because of sin, is transformed by the regenerating power of the Spirit of God.' *The Christian View of Man*, pp. 139–144. See also the full discussion in L. Berkhof's *Systematic Theology*, pp. 191–194.

*V*14: **Seeing then that we have a great high priest, that is passed into the heavens, Jesus the Son of God, let us hold fast our profession.**

**Having then a great high priest,** (RV) 'Then' is not deductive, but simply serves to introduce the Epistle's main theme, which is to show the superiority of Christ's heavenly priesthood over that earthly succession which it has completely superseded. [*Heb* 4:14–10:18] The assertion is at once a word of encouragement and an emphatic reply to the taunts of their unbelieving kinsmen who would assail the validity and efficacy of this 'new' religion on the ground that it had no high priest to intercede for its misguided adherents. Many still cannot rise to the spiritual reality of New Testament truth and must needs worship a visible Vicar of Christ on earth who blasphemously arrogates to himself the title of 'Pontifex Maximus' – the greatest High Priest! [2 *Thess* 2:4]

**who hath passed through the heavens, Jesus the Son of God,** (RV) The appearing of Jesus in glory affords convincing proof that His sacrifice was acceptable to God and assures His people of the prevailing power of His intercession on their behalf. However, this same Jesus is none other than the Son of God for our author does not speak of the conferment of divine honours upon a mere man, but plainly refers to the exaltation of Him who is natively and essentially the eternal Son. [1 *Tim* 3:16 AV] A. R. Fausset comments on the significance of the preposition used here: 'These heavens were the veil which our High Priest *passed through* into the heaven of heavens, the immediate presence of God; just as the Levitical high priest passed through the veil into the holy of holies. Neither Moses nor even Joshua could bring us into this rest; but Jesus, our Forerunner, already spiritually, hereafter in actual presence, body, soul, and spirit, brings His people into the heavenly rest.'

**let us hold fast our confession.** (RV) It is a characteristic of the author's style to include himself in his exhortations. [cf. 4:1; 4:11; 4:16; 6:1; 10:22; 10:23; 10:24; 12:1 (twice); 12:28; 13:13; 13:15] They must at all costs maintain their subjective confidence in Jesus the Son of God or else they will never participate in the objective benefits of His great salvation. [*Heb* 2:1; 6:6]

*V*15: **For we have not an high priest which cannot be touched with the feeling of our infirmities; but was in all points tempted like as we are, yet without sin.**

The double negative is equal to a strong affirmation. In case the contemplation of the Son's glory should lead them to suppose that He had no capacity for sympathy, they are given the immediate assurance that in Jesus they have a compassionate High Priest who has fully shared their 'infirmities.' Bengel turns the ambiguity of this word to good account by saying that as it applies to us it includes sin, but in regard to Christ it is excluded. (cited by T. C. Hammond, *The One Hundred Texts*, p. 219) 'The Son of God, had He never become incarnate, might have pitied, but He could not have sympathized with His people. . . . The truth is, He not only can be touched, but cannot but be touched. The assertion is not, It is possible that He may sympathize; but, It is impossible that He should not.' (John Brown)

**without sin.** The meaning is not that Jesus triumphed over temptation, though that is of course true, but that 'His sinless nature contained nothing that responded to temptation, as does ours.' (B. F. C. Atkinson, quoted by F. F. Bruce) [*John* 14:30] The sinner who capitulates to the first solicitation to evil cannot claim to have felt the full power of temptation. It was otherwise with Jesus who experienced the anguish of temptation to an unimaginable degree, for His immaculate person was subjected to the continuous assaults of the Tempter.

Thus, having suffered 'being tempted, he is able to succour them that are tempted.' [*Heb* 2:18]

*V*16: **Let us therefore come boldly unto the throne of grace, that we may obtain mercy, and find grace to help in time of need.**

**Let us therefore draw near** (RV) 'Christianity is not a DOULEIA, but a LATREIA, that is, a direct worship of God. This is intended in the sense of drawing near to God and worshipping Him. . . . The term used for this is PROSERCHESTHAI, *to draw near*, as specifically conceived. We have here specifically ritual language. Note, for example, 4:16; 7:25; 10:1, 22. This language is used not only of the believers, but also of the officers in the sanctuary, that is, of the priests. Back of this stands the idea that the priest *brings near* his sacrifice, as well as *bringing near* those who follow him. So we are brought near by Jesus as our High Priest and Forerunner.' (G. Vos)

**with boldness** (RV) ' "Boldness" is here not opposed to godly fear, but to slavish dread.' (John Brown)

**unto the throne of grace**, 'God's throne is become so to us, through the mediation of our High Priest at God's right hand. (*ch* 8:1; 12:2) Pleading Jesus' meritorious death, we shall always find God on a *throne of grace*.' (A. R. Fausset)

**that we may obtain mercy, and find grace to help** ' "Mercy" is the love that helps the wretched, "grace" the love that pardons the guilty. "Mercy" is placed first because our weaknesses have been stressed.' (Lenski)

**in time of need.** '– "seasonably": before we are overwhelmed by temptations, when we most need it; such as is suitable to the time, persons, and end designed. [*Ps* 104:27] A supply of grace is in store for believers against all exigencies; but they are only supplied with it, according as the need arises.' (A. R. Fausset)

# CHAPTER FIVE

*V*1: **For every high priest taken from among men is ordained for men in things pertaining to God, that he may offer both gifts and sacrifices for sins:**

In verses 1–4 it is shown that the Jewish High Priest must have a compassionate concern for those he represents before God, and that the effectiveness of his ministrations on their behalf rests upon the reality of a divine call to undertake this office. These requirements were perfectly met in Christ who became the High Priest of His people by divine appointment, and who is qualified to sympathize with them by His unique experience of suffering on their behalf. (*vv* 5–10)

**For every high priest, being taken from among men, is appointed for men in things pertaining to God,** (RV) The mediation of Christ depended on His kinship with those He came to redeem, for in order to manage the religious interests *of* men, every High Priest was to be 'taken *from among* men.' [*Heb* 2:9–18]

**that he may offer both gifts and sacrifices for sins:** John Owen says that 'the proper and principal work of a priest' is the offering of those 'gifts and sacrifices' which sin made necessary, and therefore 'where there is no proper propitiatory sacrifice there is no proper priest.' He also makes the following points concerning man's dire need of a divine High Priest.

'1st. *Before the entrance of sin, there was no need of the office of priesthood between God and man.*

'2dly. *Sin being entered into the world, there was no more worship to be performed immediately unto God.*

'3dly. That the worship of God might be restored again in the world, *it was indispensably necessary that some one must interpose between sinners and the holy God.*

'4thly. In this condition *no creature could undertake the office of being a priest for the church of God, which now consisted all of sinners.*

'5thly. The Son of God undertakes to be this priest for sinners: "We have a great high priest, Jesus the Son of God."' [*Heb* 4:14]

*V*2: **Who can have compassion on the ignorant, and on them that are out of the way; for that he himself also is compassed with infirmity.**

*V*3: **And by reason hereof he ought, as for the people, so also for himself, to offer for sins.**

These verses indirectly assert the superiority of Christ's Priesthood. For the Jewish High Priest must first offer for his own sins before he acted on behalf of the people, and it was this knowledge of his own infirmity which enabled him to 'bear gently with the ignorant and erring.' (RV) He ought to have a fellow-feeling for those he represents because he is himself a sinner, but this measured mildness cannot be compared with the unlimited sympathy which the sinless Son of God feels for those who have wandered from the way. [*Heb* 4:15]

*V*4: **And no man taketh this honour unto himself, but he that is called of God, as was Aaron.**

The author here pointedly reminds his readers that in contrast to the corruption of the priestly office in contemporary Judaism, Israel's first High Priest exercised a valid ministry because he was commissioned by God for this service; whereas all worship which is offered without a divine command is performed without divine approval and incurs divine judgment. [2 *Chron* 26:16–21] 'As it is the promise of God to govern the Church, so He reserves to Himself alone the right to lay down the order and manner of its administration. On this I found the principle that the papal priesthood is a spurious one, because it was fabricated in a human workshop. God nowhere commands that a sacrifice should now be offered to Him for the forgiveness of sins. He nowhere ordains that priests should be appointed for this purpose. Therefore when the Pope instals his priests to make sacrifices, the apostle says that they are not to be considered lawful unless perchance by some new and special law they exalted themselves above Christ, who Himself did not dare to take this honour on Himself, but waited for the Word of the Father.' (Calvin)

*V5*: **So also Christ glorified not himself to be made an high priest; but he that said unto him, Thou art my Son, to day have I begotten thee.**

In the same way Christ did not advance Himself to the position of High Priest, but was appointed to this office by the Father. [*John* 8:54] When Christ took His rightful place in heaven, God proclaimed Him to be His Son, and it is His essential Sonship which qualifies Him to exercise such a perpetual priesthood. Yet Christ's triumphant enthronement did not mark the beginning of His priesthood, for this divine testimony was but the public announcement of that eternal decree by which He was ordained the Mediator of His people. And it was in Christ's priestly offering of Himself upon the Cross that this decree passed into the realm of historical accomplishment. This is the second time that *Psalm* 2:7 is quoted, see also the comment on *ch* 1:5.

*V6*: **As he saith also in another place, Thou art a priest for ever after the order of Melchisedec.**

That God declared Christ to be a priest is confirmed by an appeal to *Psalm* 110:4 which also indicates that He belongs to a different order of priesthood from that of Aaron. As the promised deliverer is shown to be a prince of David's line in the first verse of the same psalm, it is evident that He can lay no claim to the priestly functions which pertained exclusively to the house of Levi. (Cited in *ch* 1:13) However, Christ's priesthood infinitely transcends the Levitical order for it is patterned upon the unique precedent afforded by Melchisedec, the Priest-King of Salem, and the Messiah therefore permanently unites in His own person the two offices which were always distinct in Israel. [*Gen* 14:18]

*V7*: **Who in the days of his flesh, when he had offered up prayers and supplications with strong crying and tears unto him that was able to save him from death, and was heard in that he feared;**

The author turns next to the experience of suffering which fitted Christ to be a sympathetic High Priest. (*vv* 7–9) While the phrase 'who in the days of his flesh,' would seem to refer to the whole period of His humiliation, the rest of the verse appears to point to his agony in Gethsemane. 'These prayers, accompanied with strong crying and tears, to Him who was able to save Him from death, imply the endurance of penal death. Did he fear the mere corporeal suffering which many a martyr has met with fortitude? Sinless nature no doubt shrinks from death, but it was something of a far other quality which gave rise to the agony and amazement which weighed so heavily on the Son of God, – viz., the second death, the full infliction of wrath at the hand of God for the sins, not of one man, but of the whole company of the elect. The curse of the law under which He spontaneously placed Himself struck the soul as well as the body. [*Gal* 3:13] More was comprehended than bodily pain, as might be argued from the horror and recoil of the Redeemer from the cup which was to be drunk. Besides, corporeal sufferings would not have sufficed for men's redemption, for He redeemed the soul as well as the body [1 *Cor* 6:20]: He assumed both soul and body; and He offered both in our room, as was necessary to expiate guilt incurred in both and by both. . . . Hence, while the Lord Jesus continued amid all His agony the object of divine love as the only-begotten of the Father, He endured all the curse, wrath, and infliction justly to be awarded to the sin He bore on His own body. . . . Though the Surety was in Himself the beloved Son, He was, as the sin-bearer, under the hiding of His Father's face when He poured out these prayers with strong crying and tears.' (G. Smeaton)

Now it is said that these supplications were answered because of 'his godly fear.' (rv) Yet how can this statement be reconciled with the fact that He died? The solution of this difficulty is found in the conditional nature of the prayers which Christ offered, for though He could not but wish that the cup might pass from Him, nevertheless He submitted Himself entirely to the Father's will, and it was this definite petition which was fully granted. [*Matt* 26:39; *Mark* 14:36; *Luke* 22:42]

## *V*8: **Though he were a Son, yet learned he obedience by the things which he suffered;**

The Son's eternal equality with the Father placed Him above all obedience, but the point which is emphasized here is His willingness to become obedient unto death, 'even the death of

[64]

the cross', for the sake of those He came to save. [*Gal* 4:4, 5; *Phil* 2:6–8] Here '*learning obedience* signifies *bringing out into the present conscious experience of action* that which was already present in principle. There is a great difference, of course, between the mere principle and even the desire to obey, and the actual carrying out of the desire.' (G. Vos) [*Heb* 10:7]

*V*9: **And being made perfect, he became the author of eternal salvation unto all them that obey him;**

**And having been made perfect,** (RV) 'As to the term *perfection* (TELEIŌSIS), we must adhere strictly to the meaning *fitting for the office*. The experience of learning was a moral experience, to be sure; but the perfection attained was not moral perfection, but a perfect fitness for His office.' (G. Vos)

**he became the author of eternal salvation** Thus Christ's triumph over suffering secured the eternal salvation of His people. In *Hebrews* 2:10 Christ 'is called the captain or leader of salvation, the first in the order of possession; whereas in this passage He is called the meritorious cause, the author of salvation.' (G. Smeaton)

**unto all them that obey him.** A genuine participation in this salvation is always attested by an obedient walk. '*All*, whether Jew or Gentile, "who obey Him" shall be saved by Him. *None* who do not obey Him shall be saved by Him. There is, there can be, no salvation through Christ to men living and dying in unbelief, impenitence, and disobedience.' (John Brown)

*V*10: **Called of God an high priest after the order of Melchisedec.**
**Named of God a high priest after the order of Melchizedek.** (RV)

'Having been made perfect' Christ entered the heavenly sanctuary and was greeted by God as the High Priest of a more excellent order than that of Aaron. The significance of this designation is explained in the seventh chapter of the Epistle. 'God nameth or calleth things as they are, and as he hath made them; and this was done openly, and with the most illustrious solemnity, at his ascension into heaven, when God set him down on his right hand in the presence of all the surrounding angels, who did all submit to him as their Head and King, and acknowledge him as the great royal High Priest of God, as was foretold.' (Poole) [Ps 110:1, 4]

V11: **Of whom we have many things to say, and hard to be uttered, seeing ye are dull of hearing.**

The closing word of the previous verse marks a skilful transition from instruction to an extended exhortation. [Heb 5:11–6:20] He has much to say to them concerning Melchisedec as a type of Christ, but he fears that the sluggishness of their hearing offers an insuperable impediment to the doctrine which he wishes to deliver to them. [Heb 6:12] The obscurity does not reside in the teaching but in that spiritual insensitivity which is the invariable concomitant of coldness of heart. This crushing rebuke is therefore intended to arouse them from their torpor so that his words may not uselessly fall upon deaf ears.

V12: **For when for the time ye ought to be teachers, ye have need that one teach you again which be the first principles of the oracles of God; and are become such as have need of milk, and not of strong meat.**

The charge is substantiated by the reminder that their progress in the faith bears no relation to what might have been justly expected from the time that they have professed it. To judge from this they ought now to be teachers, whereas they still needed to be taught the very rudiments of the faith, and had to be fed with milk because they were unable to digest solid food. [cf. 1 *Cor* 3:1 ff.]

**of the oracles of God** '– viz., of the Old Testament. Instead of seeing Christ as the end of the Old Testament, they were relapsing towards Judaism, so as not only not to understand the typical reference to Christ of such an Old Testament personage as Melchisedec, but even more elementary references.' (A. R. Fausset)

*V*13: **For every one that useth milk is unskilful in the word of righteousness: for he is a babe.**

Their spiritual immaturity was evidenced by the fact that they were restricted to a diet of milk, and so they were 'without experience of the word of righteousness.' (RV) The context would seem to rule out any reference to justification, and the expression is probably to be understood as a synonym for the Christian faith. Arndt-Gingrich point out that as righteousness 'constitutes the specific virtue of Christians, the word becomes almost equivalent to Christianity.'

*V*14: **But strong meat belongeth to them that are of full age, even those who by reason of use have their senses exercised to discern both good and evil.**

On the other hand, 'solid food is for full-grown men' (RV) whose experience enables them to discriminate between what is good and what is harmful. The lesson is plain to see: as indolence accounted for their lamentable ignorance of Christian truth, so every faculty must be kept in vigorous exercise to ensure healthy spiritual growth. [*Prov* 13:4]

# CHAPTER SIX

**VI: Therefore leaving the principles of the doctrine of Christ, let us go on unto perfection; not laying again the foundation of repentance from dead works, and of faith toward God,**

**Therefore leaving the word of the beginning of Christ, let us go on unto perfection;** (AV margin) Accordingly, they must no longer adhere to the ceremonial law by which Christ was typically prefigured in the Old Testament 'oracles' [5:12], but rather press on to a full apprehension of the 'perfection' [5:9] of His redeeming work. [*John* 1:29] 'The apostle is not contrasting two different stages of Christianity, an infantile and a mature; rather is he opposing, once more, the substance over against the shadows. He continues to press upon the Hebrews their need of forsaking the visible for the invisible, the typical for the antitypical.' (Arthur Pink)

**not laying again the foundation** A brief enumeration of the basis of Jewish belief is preceded by a warning that this foundation is not to be re-laid, for this rudimentary teaching has been absorbed in that full and final revelation which was given to them in Christ.

**of repentance from dead works, and of faith toward God,** The Jew was taught the necessity of repentance from

CHAPTER 6 VERSE 2

those sinful works which reached their natural terminus in death. He knew that he could not be forgiven while he continued to cling to his sin. But repentance alone could not secure his restoration to divine favour, for he also knew that this must always be accompanied by faith in God's forgiving grace. [Hab 2:4] It is certain that the preparatory dispensation is in view here because Christian faith is directed towards the God who is now identified as 'the God and Father of our Lord Jesus Christ.' [1 Pet 1:3]

*V2*: **Of the doctrine of baptisms, and of laying on of hands, and of resurrection of the dead, and of eternal judgment.**

**of the teaching of washings, and of laying on of hands,** (RV margin) In the same way the lustrations of Judaism were valueless without faith's appropriation of an objective sacrifice for sin. The efficacy of these ceremonial cleansings therefore depended upon the atoning blood. The other New Testament occurrences of this word BAPTISMOS clearly show that it has no reference to Christian baptism [Mark 7:4, 8; Heb 9:10], but that it describes those ablutions prescribed by the law. [See for example, Exod 30:18, 19; Lev 16:4; Num 19:19] Thus these rites faintly foreshadowed the real purification which was effected by the blood of Christ. [Compare Lev 16:21 with 1 John 1:7, 9] This thought is beautifully expressed in a great hymn by Isaac Watts.

> 'Not all the blood of beasts
>   On Jewish altars slain
> Could give the guilty conscience peace
>   Or wash away the stain.
>
> But Christ, the heavenly Lamb,
>   Takes all our sins away;

*A sacrifice of nobler name*
*And richer blood than they.*

*My faith would lay her hand*
*On that dear head of Thine,*
*While like a penitent I stand*
*And there confess my sin.*

*Believing, we rejoice*
*To see the curse remove;*
*We bless the Lamb with cheerful voice*
*And sing His bleeding love!'*

**and of resurrection of the dead, and of eternal judgment.** Unlike the Greek, the Jew could not look upon history as a meaningless succession of moments because he was the recipient of a supernatural disclosure which assured him that all things were moving towards the consummation of God's eternal purpose. It is only the acknowledgment of this divine purpose which invests history, and therefore all human activity, with any ultimate meaning. The practical denial of this telic goal is constantly exemplified in the ethical relativism of the natural man. Felix was not terribly concerned about his conduct until Paul 'reasoned of righteousness, temperance, AND JUDGMENT TO COME,' and *then* he trembled! [*Acts* 24: 25] The resurrection of the dead was plainly taught in the Old Testament and this doctrine was closely connected with the final judgment. [*Is* 26:19; *Dan* 7:9 ff; 12:2] It is here described as 'eternal judgment' in order to distinguish it 'from the temporal judgments of the present age.' (F. F. Bruce)

*V*3: **And this will we do, if God permit.**

**if God permit.** Although it is the author's desire to teach them 'the way of God more perfectly' he fears that perhaps their unbelief had so provoked God that He would not grant them further light. Even the sun's meridian splendour brings no illumination to sightless eyes! [*Luke* 8:18] 'If God give me life and ability, and you capacity and stability; for many fall away, whose damnation sleepeth not.' (Trapp)

*V4*: **For it is impossible for those who were once enlightened, and have tasted of the heavenly gift, and were made partakers of the Holy Ghost,**

*V5*: **And have tasted the good word of God, and the powers of the world to come,**

*V6*: **If they shall fall away, to renew them again unto repentance; seeing they crucify to themselves the Son of God afresh, and put him to an open shame.**

This very severe warning is intended to arouse the readers to a lively sense of the awful danger which faced them, for what they calmly considered to be a return to the faith of their fathers is shown as an act of apostasy from which no recovery is possible. The author hopes to recall them from the brink of disaster by an alarming description of those who totally fall away from the profession of the Christian faith. (*v* 9) This class of persons once appeared to be truly regenerate but their subsequent course sadly proved that they had 'neither part nor lot in this matter.' [*Acts* 8:21]

**for those who were once enlightened,** This refers to their acceptance of the doctrine of the gospel, for unless they had first professed its truth they could not have fallen away from it. [*John* 2:19] 'The sin against the Holy Ghost, though similar, is not identical with this; for *that* may be committed by those *outside* the church [as in *Matt* 12:24, 31, 32]; *this*, only by those *inside*.' (A. R. Fausset)

[71]

**and have tasted of the heavenly gift,** '*There is a goodness and excellency in this heavenly gift which may be tasted or experienced in some measure by such as never receive them in their life, power, and efficacy.* They may taste, – 1. Of the *word* in its truth, not its power; 2. Of the *worship* of the church in its outward order, not in its inward beauty; 3. Of the *gifts* of the church, not its graces.' (Works of John Owen, *On the Nature and Causes of Apostasy,* Vol. VII, p. 25) [*Matt* 7:22, 23; *Mark* 6:20; *Luke* 10:17–20; *John* 6:70]

**and were made partakers of the Holy Ghost,** 'not by an inhabitation of his person in them, but by his operations in them, whereby he is trying how far a natural man may be raised, and not have his nature changed . . . He is proving by his gifts to them how much supernatural good, and workings towards salvation, they are capable of, without the putting forth of the exceeding greatness of his power to make them new creatures.' (Poole) [*2 Pet* 2:20–22]

**And have tasted the good word of God, and the powers of the world to come,** The powers of the world to come are projected into the present age through the ministry of the Spirit in the proclamation of the Word of God. The preaching of the good news is therefore a foretaste of the heavenly state.

**If they shall fall away,** or rather, **And then fell away,** (RV) This fall is final and without remedy. The faith of God's elect endures to the end; temporary faith withers and dies. [*Matt* 13:20–22]

**For it is impossible . . . to renew them again to repentance;** The impossibility resides in the apostates themselves, for the complete repudiation of the doctrine which formerly they embraced means that a further preaching of the gospel would be entirely lost upon them. [*Matt* 7:6]

[72]

**seeing they crucify to themselves the Son of God afresh, and put him to an open shame.** 'The apostate crucifies Christ on his own account by virtually confirming the judgment of the actual crucifiers, declaring that he, too, has made trial of Jesus and found Him no true Messiah but a deceiver and therefore worthy of death.' (*Expositor's Greek Testament*, cited by K. Wuest) Thus the heinous nature of their sin makes repentance impossible.

*V*7: **For the earth which drinketh in the rain that cometh oft upon it, and bringeth forth herbs meet for them by whom it is dressed, receiveth blessing from God:**

*V*8: **But that which beareth thorns and briers is rejected, and is nigh unto cursing; whose end is to be burned.**

A telling illustration from the realm of nature sets forth the solemn truth that the hearing of the gospel is fraught with eternal consequences for either weal or woe. The land which is blessed by God with frequent showers of rain is expected to bear useful fruits for those by whom it is tended, but that which produces only thorns and thistles is rejected and destined to utter destruction.

**whose end is to be burned.** 'The end of briers and thorns is the fire, they are to be burnt up by it; and this will be the final issue with apostates, to be destroyed by a Christ whom they have rejected, with eternal fire, *ch* 10:27; 12:29; *Matt* 3:12; 25:41; *2 Thess* 1:7–9.' (Poole)

*V*9: **But, beloved, we are persuaded better things of you, and things that accompany salvation, though we thus speak.**

By means of this affectionate address the author seeks to assure his readers that his stern admonition was prompted by a sincere concern for their spiritual welfare, and though 'he had spoken it *unto them*, he did not speak it *of them*.' (John Owen) For he had every reason to hope that the past evidences they had given of their faith indicated something more than an empty profession. The assurance is in no sense a retraction of the warning, but is rather intended to dispel any prejudice which might prevent it from having the desired effect upon them. 'Beloved' is used only here in the Epistle.

*V*10: **For God is not unrighteous to forget your work and labour of love, which ye have shewed toward his name, in that ye have ministered to the saints, and do minister.**

**For God is not unrighteous to forget your work and the love which ye shewed toward his name,** (RV) Since God is not unfaithful to His promise he cannot fail to recompense the service which a reverence for His name inspired, yet this is the award of grace, and not a merited reward. [*Luke* 17:10] 'The butler may forget Joseph, and Joseph forget his father's house; but forgetfulness befalls not God, to whom all things are present, and before whom there is written a book of remembrance for them that fear the Lord, and think upon his name, *Mal* 3:17.' (Trapp)

**in that ye ministered unto the saints, and still do minister.** (RV) In ministering to their fellow-believers in distress they showed their interest in the gospel, for 'those brethren who, being loved in and for God, do evidence to these Hebrews that they are passed from death to life, 1 *John* 3:14.' (Poole)

*V*11: **And we desire that every one of you do shew the same diligence to the full assurance of hope unto the end:**

*V*12: **That ye be not slothful, but followers of them who through faith and patience inherit the promises.**

However, he hopes that a consideration of the end of those who relinquish their profession will prove so salutary that each of them will be stimulated to a diligent exercise of that assurance which leads to the realization of the Christian hope. He does not wish them to become 'sluggish, but imitators of them who through faith and patience inherit the promises.' (RV) The use of the same word (NŌTHROS) in *ch* 5:11 shows that it was their 'dullness' in hearing which made it necessary to warn them against becoming 'sluggish' in their hope. For a careless hearing of the Word of God at first diminishes and eventually extinguishes the hope of salvation. Thus it is because the promised inheritance can only be possessed by those who entertain a living hope that they are urged to emulate the patience and perseverance of their forefathers whose faith is so eloquently commended in the eleventh chapter of the Epistle.

*V*13: **For when God made promise to Abraham, because he could swear by no greater, he sware by himself,**

*V*14: **Saying, Surely blessing I will bless thee, and multiplying I will multiply thee.**

*V*15: **And so, after he had patiently endured, he obtained the promise.**

God condescended to confirm with an oath the promise He made to Abraham, for though this could add nothing to the trustworthiness of His word, yet it comforted Abraham to have it so emphatically endorsed. But since there is none greater than God the only way in which He could take such an oath was to swear by Himself, a precedent which incidentally attests the legitimate use of oaths in human relations.

Although Abraham knew that the earlier promise of a numerous posterity depended for its fulfilment upon the child of his old age, yet he would not withhold even his only son from God, and this unquestioning obedience was rewarded by the solemn ratification of the promise, the substance of which is reproduced in verse 14. [*Gen* 12:2 f.; 22:16 f.; *Heb* 11:19] Abraham received a partial fulfilment of the promise in this life, and at death entered more fully into its blessings. [*Matt* 8: 11; *John* 8:56] Thus the Hebrews are reminded of the illustrious example of their revered progenitor in order to encourage them in the exercise of that patient endurance which leads to the possession of the promised salvation.

*V*16: **For men verily swear by the greater: and an oath for confirmation is to them an end of all strife.**

'This shows (1.) an oath is sanctioned even in the Christian dispensation; (2.) the limits to its use are, that it only be employed where it can *put an end to contradiction in disputes,* and *for confirmation* of a solemn promise.' (A. R. Fausset)

*V*17: **Wherein God, willing more abundantly to shew unto the heirs of promise the immutability of his counsel, confirmed it by an oath:**

So God 'interposed with an oath' (RV) to assure Abraham's spiritual heirs of His unchangeable resolve to secure their salvation. [*Rom* 8:17; *Gal* 3:22, 26, 29; 4:26–28; *Heb* 1:14] 'His word is sufficient, yet tendering our infirmity he hath bound it with an oath, and set to his seal. His word cannot be made more true, but yet more credible. Now two things make a thing more credible: 1. The quality of the person speaking; 2. The manner of the speech. If God do not simply speak, but solemnly swear, and seal to us remission of sins, and adoption of sons by the broad seal of the sacraments, and by the privy seal of his Spirit, should we not rest assured?' (Trapp)

*V18:* **That by two immutable things, in which it was impossible for God to lie, we might have a strong consolation, who have fled for refuge to lay hold upon the hope set before us:**

The complete veracity of God's word is at once a grand incentive to persevere in the hope which they had embraced and a tacit rebuke for their tendency to waver in that hope. The bare promise of God should be sufficient to command their belief, but when it is reinforced by His oath the complete impropriety of continuing to doubt the One for whom 'it is impossible to lie' is apparent. Thus these 'two immutable' assurances afford the strongest possible encouragement to remain steadfast in their profession.

**who have fled for refuge to lay hold upon the hope set before us:** Whatever may be the precise meaning of this metaphor it is plain that it refers to the protection which the Christian hope provides against an impending calamity. A burning conviction of the fearful reality of the final judgment saved the first preachers of the gospel from any sense of embarrassment as they solemnly warned their hearers to 'flee from the wrath to come.' Although there may be an allusion here to the cities of refuge mentioned in *Numbers* 35, the context appears to favour a nautical reference. Thus F. F. Bruce comments, 'We are refugees from the sinking ship of this present world-order, so soon to disappear; our hope is fixed in the eternal order, where the promises of God are made good to His people in perpetuity.'

*V19:* **Which hope we have as an anchor of the soul, both sure and stedfast, and which entereth into that within the veil;**

*V*20: **Whither the forerunner is for us entered, even Jesus, made an high priest for ever after the order of Melchisedec.**

'The words "sure and steadfast," and "entering within the veil," refer, we think, directly to the hope of the Christian, and are not to be considered as qualities of the *anchor*, to which it is figuratively compared. . . . The leading idea seems to be – This hope rests on Christ. He is in heaven – the perfected High Priest, "the Author of eternal salvation to all that obey Him." Hope, conducted by faith, passes through these heavens into the heaven of heavens – "enters within the veil," and confidently trusts in *Him* who is there as our "Forerunner," who has entered on our account, for our advantage, as our representative.' (John Brown) The repetition of the word 'Melchisedec' marks an adroit return to the point at which this digression began [5:10], and introduces the teaching which was promised on this theme. [5:11; 7:1 f.]

# CHAPTER SEVEN

*V*1: **For this Melchisedec, king of Salem, priest of the most high God, who met Abraham returning from the slaughter of the kings, and blessed him;**

*V*2: **To whom also Abraham gave a tenth part of all; first being by interpretation King of righteousness, and after that also King of Salem, which is, King of peace;**

*V*3: **Without father, without mother, without descent, having neither beginning of days, nor end of life; but made like unto the Son of God; abideth a priest continually.**

The author now explains how Christ's Priesthood is typically set forth in the brief appearance of the mysterious figure who blessed Abraham after his victory over the four kings, and to whom he paid tithes. [*Gen* 14:18–20; *Heb* 5:6, 10]

**For this Melchisedec . . . abideth a priest continually.** The real import of this statement is found in the intervening description and interpretation of that historic meeting. It does not mean that Melchisedec exercises an eternal priesthood which rivals that of Christ, but indicates that 'Melchisedec *remains* in so far as the type remains in the antitype, his priesthood, in Christ.' (Tholuck cited by Fausset)

John Owen insists upon the fundamental importance of this

surprising disclosure for a true understanding of the Person and Work of Christ. 'The first personal instituted type of Christ was a priest; this was Melchisedec. – There were before *real* instituted types of his work, as sacrifices; and there were *moral* types of his person, as Adam, Abel, and Noah, which represented him in sundry things; but the first person who was solemnly designed to teach and represent him, by what he was and did, was a priest. And that which God taught herein was, that the foundation of all that the Lord Christ had to do in and for the church was laid in his priestly office, whereby he made atonement and reconciliation for sin. Every thing else that he doth is built on the supposition hereof. And we must begin in the application where God begins in the exhibition. An interest in the effects of the priestly office of Christ is that which in the first place we ought to look after. This being attained, we shall be willing to be taught and ruled by him, and not else.'

**Verse 1, 2a.** In spite of the degenerate polytheism of his neighbours, the sacred narrative describes Melchisedec as a 'priest of God Most High' (RV), a designation which distinguishes him as a servant of the only true God. He also ruled over the city of Salem, which is almost certainly to be identified with Jerusalem. Moreover, even the patriarch Abraham freely acknowledged the greatness of this man by whom he was blessed (*v* 7), and to whom he gave 'the tenth of the spoils.' (*v* 4)

**Verse 2b.** The author finds a typical significance in the words 'Melchisedec' and 'Salem,' for the first means 'King of righteousness' while the second refers to the blessings of 'peace' which flow from his righteous rule. This is ever the order with God. The peace which is enjoyed by those who dwell in Salem is based upon the justifying righteousness of their great Priest-King. [*Jer* 23:6]

**Verse 3.** In this verse the reasoning proceeds on the premise that even the silence of Scripture is pregnant with meaning. 'Melchizedek was an historical person and not eternal, still as a Scriptural figure he was regarded as eternal, being without recorded father or mother or genealogy, and having no recorded beginning of days nor end of life. In these respects he is like unto the Son of God, that is, stripped of all earthly attachments. As such, then, he is also a type of Christ. Thus *as he appears in Scripture* he may be regarded as enveloped in an atmosphere of eternity.' (G. Vos) The refusal to see anything in Melchisedec save that which is taught in Scripture leads Calvin to conclude that, 'In dealing with everything that has to do with Christ we must scrupulously observe that we do not accept anything that is not from the Word of God.' Unlike the Levitical priests, the priesthood of Melchisedec was not limited to a prescribed period nor did it depend for its exercise upon a carefully preserved genealogy, for his priestly office was derived from his personal dignity, and in this he resembled the Son of God. The immeasurable superiority of Christ's Priesthood over the earthly order which it replaced rests upon the divine dignity of his eternal Sonship. Hence John Owen pertinently observes, 'That Christ, abiding a priest for ever, hath no more a vicar, or successor, or substitute in his office, or any deriving a real priesthood from him, than had Melchisedec.'

*V4*: **Now consider how great this man was, unto whom even the patriarch Abraham gave the tenth of the spoils.**

These Hebrew Christians are now earnestly urged to consider an amazing spectacle: here is the respected founder of their race paying the very best of the booty to a Gentile priest! 'Abraham's doing homage to Melchisedec is a plain proof that, in his sacred chracter, Melchisedec was superior to any of the religious officers under the legal economy.' (John Brown)

*V*5: **And verily they that are of the sons of Levi, who receive the office of the priesthood, have a commandment to take tithes of the people according to the law, that is, of their brethren, though they come out of the loins of Abraham:**

*V*6: **But he whose descent is not counted from them received tithes of Abraham, and blessed him that had the promises.**

*V*7: **And without all contradiction the less is blessed of the better.**

Although they were brethren in virtue of their descent from a common ancestor, the people were obliged by the law of God to pay tithes to the sons of Levi because the priesthood belonged to them. As Melchisedec obviously had no place in the Levitical line, Abraham did not present tithes to him as a matter of legal obligation, but in voluntary recognition of his superiority as 'priest of the most high God.' In verse 6 the author draws attention to Abraham's dignity as the possessor of the divine promises in order to enhance the greatness of the One by whom he was blessed, for it is beyond dispute that 'the less is blessed of the better.'

**hath taken tithes of Abraham, and hath blessed him** (*v* 6 RV) Lenski points out that the perfect tense is used to convey 'the lasting significance and effect of these priestly acts.'

*V*8: **And here men that die receive tithes; but there he receiveth them, of whom it is witnessed that he liveth.**

This verse points a further contrast between the sons of Levi and Melchisedec, for while the former are dying men even as they receive tithes, the silence of Scripture concerning the latter's death is a positive witness to the fact that he lives. This means that the typical Priest-King of Salem lives on in the great Antitype whom he foreshadowed. 'Melchisedec "liveth" merely in his *official* capacity, his priesthood being continued in Christ. Christ is, *in His own person*, "ever-living after the power of an endless life" (*vv* 16, 25).' (A. R. Fausset)

*V*9: **And as I may so say, Levi also, who receiveth tithes, payed tithes in Abraham.**

*V*10: **For he was yet in the loins of his father, when Melchisedec met him.**

In fact 'to use just the right word' (Arndt-Gingrich), Levi 'hath paid tithes' (RV – perfect tense again) to Melchisedec in the person of the patriarch Abraham, whose acknowledgment of this priest was a representative act which involved all his descendants. Lenski enters a vigorous protest against the suggestion that this forms an apologetic conclusion to what even the author regards as an artificial argument. 'Why speak of it as being "perhaps open to objection," as "loose" and not "literal" when countless acts of ancestors are regarded in the same way today? Did Adam's act not put death upon all of us [*Rom* 5:12]? When a king abdicates, does that not count also for his sons and for their sons? When I squander my property, do my heirs still retain it? Why speak of Levi as not personally giving assent to what was done by Abraham before Levi was born? Although he was at that time unborn and gave no personal assent did Levi not share in Abraham's blessing, both that which was bestowed by God and that which was pronounced by Melchizedek?'

**in the loins of his father** '– i.e., *forefather*, Abraham. *Christ* did not pay tithes in Abraham, for He never was in the loins of an earthly father (*Alford*). Though, in respect to His mother, He was "of the fruit of (David's, and so of) Abraham's loins,"

[83]

yet, being supernaturally, without human father, conceived, as He is above the natural law of birth, so is He above the law of tithes. Those alone born naturally, and so in sin, needed to pay tithe to the priest, to make propitiation for their sin. Not so Christ, who derived only his flesh, not also the taint of the flesh, from Abraham.' (A. R. Fausset)

*V*II: **If therefore perfection were by the Levitical priesthood, (for under it the people received the law,) what further need was there that another priest should rise after the order of Melchisedec, and not be called after the order of Aaron?**

If the Levitical order had achieved the end for which the priestly office had been instituted by God, then clearly the Psalmist would not have spoken of the rise of a different kind of priest. [*Ps* 110:4] This failure is heightened by the words in parenthesis which express the idea, '*for the people were subjected to a law in reference to that priesthood.*' (John Brown) For though Israel rendered an outward obedience to the laws which regulated the service of the earthly sanctuary, yet its priests remained powerless to effect that inward cleansing of the conscience which alone could 'make the comers thereunto perfect.' [*Heb* 10:1] Hence the need of another order of priesthood was proved by the inadequacy of their ministrations.

*V*12: **For the priesthood being changed, there is made of necessity a change also of the law.**

The meaning of this assertion is well explained by John Brown. 'If a person, by divine appointment, fill the office of the priesthood who does not answer to the description given of a priest in the law – if he belongs not to the class to which, by that law, the priesthood is restricted, it is perfectly plain that He who enacted the law has annulled it. Jesus Christ's being a

Priest, is a clear proof that the Mosaic law about the priest-hood is abrogated.'

**V13 : For he of whom these things are spoken pertaineth to another tribe, of which no man gave attendance at the altar.**

**For he of whom these things are said hath partaken of another tribe,** (RV margin) As Fausset notes, 'the perfect implies the *continuance still* of His manhood.' [*Rev* 5:5] This change in the law concerning the priesthood was implied in the Psalmist's prediction, for the one of whom he spoke was excluded from offering the sacrifices prescribed under that law because he did not belong to the tribe of Levi. [*Ps* 110:1, 4] 'Seeing Christ himself had no right to minister at the material altar, the re-introduction of such altars is inconsistent with the perpetual continuance of his priesthood.' (John Owen)

**V14 : For it is evident that our Lord sprang out of Juda; of which tribe Moses spake nothing concerning priest-hood.**

**For it is evident that our Lord hath sprung out of Judah;** (RV) 'For as we very well know, *our* Lord is of the tribe of Judah!' David expressed his personal interest in the Messiah when he addressed Him as 'my Lord' [*Ps* 110:1], and Lenski suggests that the author's use of the pronoun 'our' is intended gently to recall his readers to their confession of faith in Christ. Many scriptures plainly foretold that the Messiah was to belong to the tribe of Judah [e.g. *Gen* 49:8–10; *Is* 11:1–5; *Mic* 5:2], while the words 'hath sprung' refer to the historical appearance of this promised 'Branch' [*Jer* 23:5; *Zech* 3:8; 6:12].

[85]

**as to which tribe Moses spake nothing concerning priests.** (RV) The lack of a positive appointment to the priesthood in the law of Moses excluded the men of Judah from exercising this office as effectively as if it had been expressly forbidden to them. [*Jer* 7:31; *Col* 2:20–23] 'That a ceremony is not expressly forbidden by Scripture does not warrant its practice, because the Scriptural rule excludes all religious ceremonies which are not of Divine appointment. Their not being commanded is therefore a sufficient reason for refusing them.' (Samuel Palmer, The Nonconformist's Catechism, 1773. Reprinted in *Sermons of the Great Ejection*, pp. 201–220)

*V*15: **And it is yet far more evident: for that after the similitude of Melchisedec there ariseth another priest,**

Moreover, it is still clearer that the supernatural advent of the Eternal Priest, who was foreshadowed by Melchisedec and promised through David, ensured the abolition of that priesthood which was purely temporal in character.

*V*16: **Who is made, not after the law of a carnal commandment, but after the power of an endless life.**

**who hath been made,** (RV) Christ became such a priest by the appointment of the Father. Here the priesthood which was exercised under the law of a 'fleshly' commandment is adversely compared to that which is endued with the power of an endless life.

**not after the law of a carnal commandment,** (or lit. *fleshen* commandment) 'The Law of the Aaronic priesthood had reference to descent from a particular tribe, to bodily conditions, to marriage, in a word to "flesh," a word which expresses all that which is mortal and perishable. A priesthood created and exercised under such a fleshen commandment can

CHAPTER 7 VERSES 17–18

have no effects outside of the principle which regulates it; it can never extend its influence into the region of spirit and life.' (A. B. Davidson)

**but after the power of an indissoluble life:** (RV margin) It was otherwise with Christ whose 'physical death as Man was no dissolution of His eternal life as God.' (A. M. Stibbs) And it is because this perpetual life is the inalienable possession of the Risen Christ that he is able freely to bestow it upon His people. [*Heb* 7:25]

*V*17: **For he testifieth, Thou art a priest for ever after the order of Melchisedec.**

This explicit appeal to the Word of God shows that the author does not expect these revolutionary inferences [5:11 f] to be accepted unless they are seen to be in accordance with its testimony.

**For it is witnessed of him,** (RV) 'This is proved by infallible testimony in *Psalm* 110:4, God the Father himself solemnly declared him to be so before the angels in heaven, and revealed it to men on earth by the prophet David.' (Poole)

**Thou art a priest for ever after the order of Melchisedec.** 'The alteration that God made in the church, by the introduction of the priesthood of Christ, was progressive towards its perfection. – To return, therefore, unto or look after legal ceremonies in the worship of God, is to go back unto poor, "beggarly elements" and "rudiments of the world."' (John Owen)

*V*18: **For there is verily a disannulling of the commandment going before for the weakness and unprofitableness thereof.**

*V*19: **For the law made nothing perfect, but the bringing in of a better hope did; by the which we draw nigh unto God.**

The introduction of a 'better hope,' by which *we* draw near to God [10:19–22], meant the abrogation of the 'foregoing commandment' (RV) which brought nothing to completion.

**(For the law made nothing perfect),** (RV) 'For, indeed, that law made nothing perfect. It did not make a perfect priest; it did not make perfect expiation; it did not afford perfect peace of conscience; it did not give real, far less perfect, sanctification. If it had, it would have been permanent.' (John Brown)

However, in spite of its preliminary character, the ceremonial law possessed a spiritual value because it foreshadowed the grace which was to be revealed in Christ. The rites which were practised under its provisions derived their efficacy from His forthcoming sacrifice, after which the divine authority for their continuance was withdrawn. [cf. *Matt* 27:51 with *Heb* 10:19, 20] Therefore those who still continued to cling to the shadow actually forfeited the substance it had once represented.

*V*20: **And inasmuch as not without an oath he was made priest:**

*V*21: **(For those priests were made without an oath; but this with an oath by him that said unto him, The Lord sware and will not repent, Thou art a priest for ever after the order of Melchisedec:)**

Moreover, the selfsame scripture provides a further proof of the superiority of this priesthood by its revelation of God's eternal decree in this solemn oath. From this it is evident that

Christ must be a priest forever because the purpose of God is immutable. The fact that no such oath was made in connection with the Levitical order showed the temporary nature of their service, for the legal dispensation was but a preparation for the advent of the Promised Seed. [*Gal* 3:17–27]

*V*22: **By so much was Jesus made a surety of a better testament.**

**By so much also hath Jesus become the surety of a better covenant.** (RV) The sentence which was broken by the parenthesis of the previous verse is now completed. It is the divine oath which distinguishes Jesus (his name being placed last in the sentence for emphasis) as the surety of a better covenant (DIATHĒKĒ). The importance of this word to the author's argument may be gauged from the fact that this is the first of the seventeen times he uses it in this Epistle, whereas it only occurs another sixteen times in the rest of the New Testament. (G. Vos) R. V. G. Tasker has noted that, 'The Biblical covenants between God and man, though they call for obedience and faith on man's part, are essentially divine dispositions, manifestations of His saving grace. In these covenants, though there are two parties, there is one disposer.' (*The Gospel in the Epistle to the Hebrews*, p. 16)[1] However, though the Mosaic Covenant was good, this is *better* because the fulfilment of its promises is not suspended upon the obedience and faith of its beneficiaries, for even these were purchased for them by their Surety. [*Ps* 110:3; *Heb* 8:6–13] This word 'surety' (EGGUOS) appears only here in the New Testament. It means that Jesus 'is the Personal guarantee of the terms of the new and better covenant, secured on the ground of His perfect sacrifice (*v* 27).' (W. E. Vine)

[1] For a fuller explanation of the word COVENANT, see the magisterial discussion by John Murray in *The New Bible Dictionary*, pp. 264–268.

*V*23: **And they truly were many priests, because they were not suffered to continue by reason of death:**

*V*24: **But this man, because he continueth ever, hath an unchangeable priesthood.**

**truly** It is an incontrovertible fact that there were many Jewish High Priests because death always made the appointment of a successor necessary. 'A signal instance of this was given in Aaron himself, the first of them. God, to show the nature of that priesthood unto the people, and to manifest that the everlasting Priest was yet to come, commanded Aaron to die *in the sight of* all the congregation: *Num* 20:25–29!' (Arthur Pink)

But the priesthood of Christ is never-ending for *He* ever lives to exercise this office.

**unchangeable** 'Perhaps *indefectible* would be a suitable translation . . . In the one flawless Mediator we descry priesthood at its summit-level. His unique endowments exhaust the requisites of the office and invest it with ineffaceable validity.' (E. K. Simpson, cited by F. F. Bruce)

*V*25: **Wherefore he is able also to save them to the uttermost that come unto God by him, seeing he ever liveth to make intercession for them.**

**Wherefore also** (RV) It follows from the foregoing that Christ is able perfectly to secure the complete salvation of all those for whom He acts as priest. (cf. *v* 24)

**he is able to save to the uttermost** (RV) 'Those who endeavour to come unto God any other way but by Christ, as by saints and angels, may do well to consider whether they have any such office in heaven as by virtue whereof they are able to save them to the uttermost. . . . All false religion is but a choice of other things for men to place their trust in, with a neglect of Christ. And all superstition grows on the same root, in all effects or instances of it, be they great or small.' (John Owen) [*John* 14:6]

**them that draw near unto God through him,** (RV) 'Attendance unto the service, the worship of God in the gospel, is required to interest us in the saving care and power of our high priest. – Men deceive themselves, who look to be saved by him, but take no care to come to God in holy worship by him.' (John Owen)

**seeing he ever liveth to make intercession** 'He is a priest now, not to offer sacrifice but as the permanent personal embodiment of all the efficacy and virtue that accrued from the sacrifice once offered. And it is as such he ever continues to make intercession for his people. His ever-continuing and always-prevailing intercession is bound to the sacrifice once offered. But it is thus bound because it is in his capacity as the great high priest of our profession that he perfected the one and continues the other.' (John Murray, *Redemption Accomplished and Applied*, pp. 28–29)

'The New Testament does not represent Him as an *orante*, *standing* ever before the Father with outstretched arms, like the figures in the mosaics of the catacombs, and with strong crying and tears pleading our cause in the presence of a reluctant God; but as a *throned* Priest-King, asking what He will from a Father who always hears and grants His request. Our Lord's life in heaven is His prayer.' (H. B. Swete, cited by R. V. G. Tasker)

**for them** 'Christ intercedes for *all* those for whom He has made atonement, and for those *only*. This may be inferred from the limited character of the atonement, and also from such passages as *Rom* 8:34; *Heb* 7:25; 9:24, in every one of which the word "us" refers to believers.' (L. Berkhof, *Systematic Theology*, p. 404) [*John* 17:9]

*V*26: **For such an high priest became us, who is holy, harmless, undefiled, separate from sinners, and made higher than the heavens;**

**For such an high priest became us,** Because '*Unholy sinners* do stand in need of a *holy priest* and a *holy sacrifice*.' (John Owen) As Smeaton correctly observes, the various predicates which follow 'are by no means to be interpreted as properties that belonged to Him exclusively after His ascension. The first four are descriptive of what He was on earth, when brought into contact, during the discharge of His office, with sin and sinners; and only because all this belonged to Him on earth, does He continue to be all this in heaven.'

**who is holy,** As befits 'the Holy One' (i.e. the Messiah), His character is absolutely holy, and His will is in complete accord with that of the Father. [*Ps* 16:10 LXX; *Acts* 2:27; 13:35; *Heb* 10:7] Thus the *moral holiness* of Jesus far excels the *ritual purity* of the Levitical priests. (Suggested by Moffatt and cited by Hewitt)

**harmless,** His nature is 'free from every taint of evil or original sin.' (Smeaton) Or as Trapp puts it, 'Without any birth-blot.' [*Luke* 1:35]

**undefiled,** 'Undefiled signifies that He contracted no defilement amid temptations which solicited Him on every side, and that, while always in contact with sin, He continued sinless, for the infection never spread to Him.' (Smeaton)

**separate from sinners,** 'He was made *sin*, but never a *sinner*. Sinner means one who is *personally* affected by sin; Christ's person never was. He never had any fellowship with sin other than that of love and compassion, to bear it as our High Priest and Substitute.' (A. Kuyper, *The Work of the Holy Spirit*, p. 85)

**and made higher than the heavens;** 'Jesus WAS higher before [*John* 17:5], and as the *God*-MAN was *made* so by the Father after His humiliation (cf. *ch* 1:4).' (A. R. Fausset) Calvin shows the necessity for this exaltation by his remark, 'No one can unite us with God except someone who reaches to God.'

*V*27: **Who needeth not daily, as those high priests, to offer up sacrifice, first for his own sins, and then for the people's: for this he did once, when he offered up himself.**

Thus the supreme eminence of Christ's Person explains the superior efficacy of His Priesthood over that of Aaron and his successors: for, 1. their sacrifices were frequent, His was final; 2. they were sinners, He is sinless; 3. they offered animals, He offered Himself!

**for this he did once for all,** (RV) 'The passages which make mention of Christ's ONE oblation, or of His offering Himself ONCE, are conclusive as to the fact of His being a priest on earth; for that word ONCE cannot be understood of what is done in heaven. It must refer to His death as a historic fact, completed and finished here below. It is against all reason to affirm that the sacrifice was offered once, if it still continues; for the expression ONCE, or ONE OFFERING, plainly contrasts the completed sacrifice with the continuous intercession which evermore proceeds upon it. Nor does the epistle stop there: the analogy instituted between the fact that it was appointed to all men once to die, and the one atoning death of Christ (9:27), leaves us in no doubt that we must view that sacrifice as completed on the cross.' (G. Smeaton)

*V*28: **For the law maketh men high priests which have infirmity; but the word of the oath, which was since the law, maketh the Son, who is consecrated for evermore.**

The disparity is even more starkly displayed in the concluding contrast which crowns the whole argument. The law appointed men with sinful infirmities, but the word of the oath appointed a Son who has been 'perfected for evermore.' (RV) This means that 'all sacrifices had been consummated in the one Sacrifice, all priesthoods absorbed in the one Priest. The offering had been made once for all: and, as there were no more victims, there could be no more priests.' (J. B. Lightfoot, 'The Christian Ministry,' appended to *The Epistle to the Philippians*, p. 265) Therefore, 'Plurality of priests under the gospel overthrows the whole argument of the apostle in this place; and if we have yet priests that have infirmities, they are made by the law, and not by the gospel.' (John Owen)

# CHAPTER EIGHT

**VI: Now of the things which we have spoken this is the sum: We have such an high priest, who is set on the right hand of the throne of the Majesty in the heavens;**

**Now in the things which we are saying the chief point is this:** (RV) In this section of the Epistle the author compares in great detail Christ's priestly ministry with that which was exercised by mortal men. This discussion naturally rests upon what has gone before, but the main point to remember is that Christ ministers in the heavenly sanctuary and not in an earthly tabernacle made with hands. [*Heb* 9:24]

**We have such a high priest, who sat down on the right hand of the throne of the Majesty in the heavens;** (RV) 'Infinitely above all other priests in this one grand respect, He exercises His priesthood IN HEAVEN, not in the earthly "holiest place." The Levitical high priests, even when they entered the holiest once a year, only STOOD for a *brief space before the symbol* of God's throne; but Jesus SITS *on the throne* of the Divine Majesty in the heaven itself, and this *for ever* (*ch* 10:11, 12).' (A. R. Fausset)

**V2: A minister of the sanctuary, and of the true tabernacle, which the Lord pitched, and not man.**

Unlike the priests who ministered in the tabernacle which was pitched by man, Christ is a minister of the *true* tabernacle.

This statement 'does not imply that the tabernacle in the wilderness was not also most truly pitched at God's bidding, and according to the pattern which He had shown [*Exod 25*]; but only that it, and all things in it, were weak earthly copies of heavenly realities.' (R. C. Trench, *Synonyms of the New Testament*, pp. 26–27) John Owen makes a characteristically vigorous application of the truth taught here. 'The church hath lost nothing by the removal of the old tabernacle and temple, all being supplied by this sanctuary, true tabernacle, and minister thereof. – The glory and worship of the temple was that which the Jews would by no means part withal. . . . And in later ages men ceased not, until they had brought into Christianity itself a worship vying for external order, ceremony, pomp, and painting, with whatever was in the tabernacle or temple of old; coming short of it principally in this, that *that* was of God's institution for a time, *this* of the invention of weak, superstitious, and foolish men. Thus is it in the church of Rome. And a hard thing it is to raise the minds of men unto a satisfaction in things merely spiritual and heavenly. . . . But "unto them that believe Christ is precious." And this "true tabernacle," with his ministration, is more unto them than all the old pompous ceremonies and services of divine institution, much more the superstitious observances of human invention.'

*V*3 : **For every high priest is ordained to offer gifts and sacrifices: wherefore it is of necessity that this man have somewhat also to offer.**

A priest without a sacrifice is like a childless mother, for he is expressly appointed in order to make such offerings. Therefore if Christ is a priest He too must 'have somewhat also to offer.' The tense of the verb used here definitely excludes all thought of a continuous offering, and as F. F. Bruce observes, 'is consistent with our author's repeated emphasis on the singularity

of the sacrifice which Christ offered (cf. *chs* 7:27; 10:12).'
However, 'because Christ's crowning act of priesthood, His
offering of Himself, was done in relation to the actual presence
of God, and not in relation to the earthly figure sanctuary in
Jerusalem, it was, as the writer to the Hebrews saw it, done in
the true heavenly tabernacle and not in the shadow earthly one.
In other words, though Jesus died outside the city of Jerusalem,
His deed as a priestly act was done in heaven, or in the heaven-
lies, as Paul himself might have said, and not just on earth.'
(A. M. Stibbs, *The Finished Work of Christ*, p. 25) 'If any one
else can offer the body of Christ, he also is the minister of the
true tabernacle. – For the Lord Christ did no more. He did
but offer himself; and they that can offer him, do put themselves in his place.' (John Owen)

*V*4: **For if he were on earth, he should not be a priest,
seeing that there are priests that offer gifts according to
the law:**

Indeed the mere fact that Christ did not belong to the tribe of
Levi prevented him from presenting the offerings prescribed
by the law. His descent from Judah meant that he could never
officiate as a priest in the earthly sanctuary [*Heb* 7:13, 14],
though of course He acted as a priest on earth when He
'suffered without the gate' in order to sanctify the people.
[*Heb* 13:12]

*V*5: **Who serve unto the example and shadow of heavenly
things, as Moses was admonished of God when he was
about to make the tabernacle: for, See, saith he, that
thou make all things according to the pattern shewed to
thee in the mount.**

These priests ministered in the tabernacle which was but a
copy of the reality it represented. It provided only 'a pale re-

flexion' (Souter) of the heavenly things. Nevertheless it was a copy which God had commanded Moses to make, and it was this alone which invested it with spiritual meaning. But this meaning could not be conveyed to men if Moses were permitted to introduce any innovation into the worship of God, and therefore he was strictly admonished to make everything precisely according to the pattern which had been shown to him on the mount. Hence Calvin concludes, 'By thus emphasizing the rule that He has laid down, He forbids us to depart from it in the very slightest. For this reason all the forms of worship produced by men fail, and also those things which are called sacraments and yet have not come from God. . . . We must beware that in wishing to fit our own inventions to Christ we do not so change Him (as the papists do) that He becomes unlike Himself. It is not permissible for us to invent anything we like, but it belongs to God alone to show us *according to the pattern that was showed thee.*'

*V*6: **But now hath he obtained a more excellent ministry, by how much also he is the mediator of a better covenant, which was established upon better promises.**

Therefore Christ has obtained a more excellent ministry for He is the Mediator of a better covenant 'which has been (legally) enacted on the basis of better promises.' (Arndt-Gingrich) The superiority of this covenant lies in the fact that its promises are guaranteed by the perfect satisfaction which has been rendered to God by its Mediator on behalf of those he represented. [*Heb* 7:27]

**better promises** 'The promises in the first covenant pertained *mainly* to the present life. They were promises of length of days; of increase of numbers; of seed time and harvest; of national privileges; and of extraordinary peace, abundance and prosperity. That there was also the promise of eternal life, it would be wrong to doubt; but this was not the main thing. In the new covenant, however, the promise of spiritual blessings becomes the *principal* thing. The mind is directed to heaven; the heart is cheered with the hopes of immortal life; the favour of God and the anticipation of heaven are secured in the most ample and solemn manner.' (A. Barnes, quoted by Pink)

*V*7: **For if that first covenant had been faultless, then should no place have been sought for the second.**

'Every work of God is perfect, viewed in connection with the purpose which He means it to serve. In this point of view, the "first covenant" was faultless. But when viewed in the light in which the Jews generally considered it, as a saving economy, in all the extent of that word, it was not "faultless." It could not expiate moral guilt; it could not wash away moral pollution; it could not justify, it could not sanctify, it could not save. Its priesthood were not perfected – they were weak and inefficient; its sacrifices "could not take away sin," make perfect as concerning the conscience, or procure "access with freedom into the holiest of all." In one word, "it made nothing perfect." Had it been "faultless," had it served all the purposes of a saving economy – a restorative dispensation, there would have been no room for another institution.' (John Brown)

*V*8a: **For finding fault with them, he saith,**

The bold assertion of the previous verse is now skilfully substantiated by an appeal to Scripture. [*Jer* 31:31–34] 'There is a subtle delicacy of language in the insensible shifting of language from the covenant to the people. The covenant itself could hardly be said to be faultless, seeing that it failed to bind Israel to their God; but the true cause of failure lay in the character of the people, not in the law, which was holy, righteous, and good. . . . The old covenant was faulty because it did not provide for enabling the people to live up to the terms or conditions of it. *It* was faulty inasmuch as it did not sufficiently provide against *their* faultiness.' (*Expositor's Greek Testament*, quoted by K. Wuest)

**he saith,** (LEGEI) The significance of this 'subjectless' phrase is well brought out in a comment by B. B. Warfield: 'Like Philo, the author of the Epistle to the Hebrews looks upon Scripture as an oracular book, and all that it says, God says to him: and accordingly, like Philo, he adduces its words with a simple "it says," with the full implication that this "it says" is a "God says" also.' (*The Inspiration and Authority of the Bible*, p. 346)

*V*8b: **Behold, the days come, saith the Lord, when I will make a new covenant with the house of Israel and with the house of Judah:**

*V*9: **Not according to the covenant that I made with their fathers in the day when I took them by the hand to lead them out of the land of Egypt; because they continued not in my covenant, and I regarded them not, saith the Lord.**

*V*10: **For this is the covenant that I will make with the house of Israel after those days, saith the Lord; I will put my laws into their mind, and write them in their hearts: and I will be to them a God, and they shall be to me a people:**

*V*11: **And they shall not teach every man his neighbour, and every man his brother, saying, Know the Lord: for all shall know me, from the least to the greatest.**

*V*12: **For I will be merciful to their unrighteousness, and their sins and their iniquities will I remember no more.**

In this important prophecy the covenant which God made with Israel at Sinai is unfavourably compared to the New Covenant which would eventually replace it. The author has no other purpose in quoting it than to prove to his readers that its promises have been fulfilled by Christ and that His church now constitutes the New Israel of God.[1] As the terms of the Mosaic Covenant were rendered null and void by the disobedience of the people, God therefore speaks of a New Covenant which cannot be broken because it will ensure the spiritual response of those with whom it is made by providing for the internal renovation of their character. Under the gracious provisions of this covenant, God promises to inscribe His law upon the hearts of His people, who shall all know Him 'from the least to the greatest,' *for* 'their sins will I remember no more.'

1. **I will put my laws into their mind, and write them in their hearts** (*v* 10) At Sinai the proclamation of the law was accompanied by the most terrible portents, yet even this awesome disclosure did not succeed in securing Israel's obedience to its demands. [*Heb* 12:18–21] Indeed the perverse obduracy of the human heart is such that until God is pleased to renew it by His Spirit it cannot render any obedience to His law. [*Ezek* 36:26–27] 'It is clear from this how much force free will has, and what rightness there is in our nature before God renews us. We will and we choose, and we do so of our own accord, but our will is carried away by an almost raging impulse to resist God and cannot in any way submit to His justice. So it comes about that the Law is fatal and deadly for us

---

[1] O. T. Allis subjects the teaching of those who claim 'that the Christian Church is a mystery parenthesis which interrupts the fulfilment to Israel of the Kingdom prophecies of the Old Testament' to a devastating examination in his book *Prophecy and the Church*.

as long as it remains written on tablets of stone, as Paul says in 2 *Cor* 3:3. In short, we accept God's command obediently when He changes and corrects the native wickedness of our hearts by His Spirit; otherwise He will find nothing in us but evil passions and a heart wholly given to wickedness. It is clearly laid down that a new covenant is to be made by which God will write His laws on our hearts, because otherwise it will be of no effect.' (Calvin)

2. **all shall know me** (*v* 11) It is clear from the preceding promise that far more is connoted by this than mere notional knowledge *about* God. It rather speaks of that personal knowledge *of* God which is ever expressed in a practical conformity to the divine will. This knowledge is neither sacramentally conveyed through a hierarchy of self-styled priests, nor is it individually communicated in any mystical fashion apart from the Word of God. 'No new prophets appear with new messages. We have all of God's Word; and each has it in his own hand. We can by it even test those who stand up to preach and to teach it. "From their small up to their great" is correct: from our children and our catechumens up to our great theologians; God's saving revelation, complete at last, is accessible to all alike. It is the fulfilment of the prophecy of Jeremiah and of *Isa* 54:13; 11:9; *Hab* 2:14; *Joel* 2:28; cf., *John* 6:45; 1 *John* 2:20, 27.' (Lenski)

3. **their sins will I remember no more** (*v* 12 RV) The word 'for' which introduces the final promise indicates that the former blessings are based upon a full satisfaction for sin. As the Old Covenant was not ratified without the sprinkling of the blood of sacrifice, so the New Covenant could not be inaugurated without the shedding of Christ's blood. [*Exod* 24: 6–8; *Heb* 9:19–22] This is the meaning which Christ Himself attached to His death when He took the cup and told the amazed disciples, 'This cup is the new covenant in my blood, even that which is poured out for you.' [*Luke* 22:20 RV] His

willing submission to the death of the Cross was a divine necessity because the mercy of God is never exercised at the expense of His righteousness. [*Rom* 3:24–26] God could only forgive the sins of His people in a manner which was consistent with His holiness. [*Ps* 85:10] Thus it took nothing less than the blood of One who was divine to make good this promise of a free pardon for guilty sinners. [*Acts* 20:28] Moreover, the non-remembrance of their sin also implies the imputation of Christ's righteousness to their account, for when God 'forgets their sins, he will have their persons in everlasting remembrance, *Ps* 112:6.' (Poole) [*Rom* 5:18–21]

*V*13: **In that he saith, A new covenant, he hath made the first old. Now that which decayeth and waxeth old is ready to vanish away.**

**In that he said, A new (covenant), he hath made the first old.** In fixing upon this one word 'new' (KAINOS) the author here stresses the superiority of that covenant which has made the former one obsolete; whereas in *Heb* 12:24 he describes it as 'fresh' (NEOS) in point of time as compared with the ancient one it has replaced.

**But that which is becoming old and waxeth aged is nigh unto vanishing away.** (RV) If Jeremiah spoke of a 'new' covenant so long ago, how much nearer is the old order now to vanishing away? It is in a state of senile decrepitude, 'like an old, old man who is sinking into his grave. To such a thing the readers would go back if they again became Jews.' (Lenski) The sacrificial system did indeed vanish away with the destruction of the temple in AD 70. 'Thus the Sinaitic superstructure became antiquated. But its foundation, the Abrahamic covenant, was never abrogated, and still stands today, as the abiding basis of the new superstructure, the new covenant.' (Martin J. Wyngaarden, *The Future of the Kingdom in Prophecy and Fulfilment*, p. 124) [*Gal* 3:15–17]

# CHAPTER NINE

*V*1: **Then verily the first covenant had also ordinances of divine service, and a worldly sanctuary.**

**Now even the first (covenant) had ordinances of divine service, and its sanctuary, (a sanctuary) of this world.** (RV)

Now the first covenant had indeed a divinely appointed pattern of ministry and a holy place in which this service was performed. The tabernacle which God instructed Moses to make was a worldly sanctuary with a heavenly meaning, but precisely because it was so firmly fixed upon earth it could not afford access to the heavenly reality it dimly represented. [*Heb* 8:5]

*V*2: **For there was a tabernacle made; the first, wherein was the candlestick, and the table, and the shewbread; which is called the sanctuary.**

This tabernacle was 'made' in contrast to that which was 'not made with hands.' (*v* 11) No more is said of the tabernacle than is necessary to advance the author's argument. He makes no mention of the outer court but simply gives a brief description of the tent itself; the first compartment of which was the sanctuary, or 'the Holy place' (RV), and this contained the lampstand and the table of shewbread. [*Exod* 25:23–39; 37: 10–24]

**the candlestick** (LUCHNIA) W. E. Vine draws attention to the fact that this word 'is mistranslated "candlestick" in every occurrence in the A.V.' In an added note he explains why this is a serious mistake. 'There is no mention of a candle in the original either in the O.T. or in the N.T. The figure of that which feeds upon its own substance to provide its light would be utterly inappropriate. A lamp is supplied by oil, which in its symbolism is figurative of the Holy Spirit.'

*V*3: **And after the second veil, the tabernacle which is called the Holiest of all;**

*V*4: **Which had the golden censer, and the ark of the covenant overlaid round about with gold, wherein was the golden pot that had manna, and Aaron's rod that budded, and the tables of the covenant;**

*V*5: **And over it the cherubims of glory shadowing the mercyseat; of which we cannot now speak particularly.**

As there was a curtain at the entrance of the sanctuary, the veil which divided this first compartment from 'the Holy of holies' (RV) is here called 'the second veil.' The 'golden censer' was probably the altar of incense, which though it *stood* in the holy place, nevertheless '*referred* to the holy of holies.' (Ebrard) [*Exod* 30: 1–6; 40: 5] Beyond the veil lay the ark of the covenant in which were deposited the tables of testimony, Aaron's rod that budded, and the pot with manna in it, while the mercy seat, which formed the lid of this sacred chest, was overshadowed by the cherubim of glory. [*Exod* 16: 33, 34; 25: 16, 18–22; *Num* 17: 10) It is not the author's intention to speak of the individual significance of these things though doubtless he could have done so had it been within the scope of his present purpose. He chooses instead to describe what took place within this earthly tabernacle on the annual Day of Atonement.

*V6*: **Now when these things were thus ordained, the priests went always into the first tabernacle, accomplishing the service of God.**

*V7*: **But into the second went the high priest alone once every year, not without blood, which he offered for himself, and for the errors of the people:**

Although the ordinary priests served God continually in the holy place to which they enjoyed unhindered access without blood, entrance to the inner sanctuary was forbidden to all except the High Priest, but even he could enter it only once a year, and then not without the blood of sacrifice. Furthermore, 'this sacrificial blood was not finally efficacious, for fresh blood had to be shed and a fresh entry made into the holy of holies year by year.' (F. F. Bruce)

*V8*: **The Holy Ghost this signifying, that the way into the holiest of all was not yet made manifest, while as the first tabernacle was yet standing:**

By means of this restriction the Holy Spirit virtually declared that the way into the heavenly sanctuary was not open while the worship of the earthly tabernacle continued in accordance with God's appointment. This period came to an end with the death of Christ, when the rending of the temple veil was the supernatural sign that at last this barrier had been removed. [*Matt* 27:51] The author does not mean that there was no experience of gospel grace under the Old Testament, but 'that unimpeded access to the presence of God was not granted until Christ came to accomplish His sacrificial ministry.' (F. F. Bruce)

*V9*: **Which was a figure for the time then present, in which were offered both gifts and sacrifices, that could not make him that did the service perfect, as pertaining to the conscience;**

[106]

**Which is a parable for the time now present;** (RV) This is adduced to convince the readers of the futility of returning to a system that brought nothing to perfection, for the gifts and sacrifices which were offered in connection with the earthly tabernacle could never make 'the worshipper' (RV) complete because in themselves they possessed no power to cleanse his conscience. (cf. 9:14) Although they sufficed to secure his ceremonial purity, they were a means of grace only insofar as they pointed forward to the final sacrifice of Christ. 'Nothing can give perfect peace of conscience with God but what can make atonement for sin. And whoever attempt it any other way but by virtue of that atonement, will never attain it, in this world nor hereafter.' (John Owen)

*V*10: **Which stood only in meats and drinks, and divers washings, and carnal ordinances, imposed on them until the time of reformation.**

Moreover, the carnal service of the worldly sanctuary gave evidence of its provisional character, for these rites were only imposed until 'the time of the new order.' (Arndt-Gingrich) [Acts 15:10] The arrival of the promised Seed meant that those who still rashly continued to observe these ordinances did so without a divine warrant and in consequence were left with nothing but the empty husks of a superseded ritual.

*V*11: **But Christ being come an high priest of good things to come, by a greater and more perfect tabernacle, not made with hands, that is to say, not of this building;**

However, if the earthly tabernacle promised 'good things to come,' the actual attainment of these heavenly blessings depended entirely upon the triumphant entrance of our great High Priest into that sanctuary which is not of this world because it is not made with hands. [*Acts* 7:48, 17:24] The official designation 'Christ' not only draws attention to the Messianic fulfilment of the things thus typically promised, but also indicates the representative nature of His entry into heaven by which the salvation of His people is assured. For God's acceptance of the person of the appointed Mediator is the indisputable proof of the efficacy of the sacrifice He had offered on their behalf.

## V12: Neither by the blood of goats and calves, but by his own blood he entered in once into the holy place, having obtained eternal redemption for us.

The blood of goats and calves brought the Jewish High Priests only once a year into the holy place of the earthly tabernacle, but it was 'through his own blood' that Christ entered 'once for all' into heaven itself. (RV) 'He entered in not with, but "through his own blood", that is, by means of, or because of, His death as Man, when His human blood was shed. So, in the heavenly glory, He does not sprinkle, and never has actually sprinkled, blood upon some heavenly mercy-seat.' (A. M. Stibbs, *The Meaning of the Word 'Blood' in Scripture*, p. 18) The remarks of John Owen on the verse are to the same effect. 'It is a vain speculation, contrary to the analogy of faith, and destructive of the true nature of the oblation of Christ, and inconsistent with the dignity of his person, that he should carry with him into heaven a part of that material blood which was shed for us on the earth. This some have invented, to maintain a comparison in that wherein is none intended. The design of the apostle is only to declare by virtue of what he entered as a priest into the holy place. And this was by virtue of his own blood when it was shed, when he offered himself unto God.' Yet it is this unscriptural idea which is given support by the RSV, 'taking . . . his own blood,' an inexcusable inaccuracy which is justly criticized by both F. F. Bruce and T. Hewitt.

**having obtained eternal redemption.** (RV) What Christ obtained by His death was 'an eternal ransoming.' (Lenski) However, He did not die to secure nothing more than the possible redemption of all men, but rather 'to give his life a ransom for *many*.' [*Mark* 10:45] 'It is to beggar the concept of redemption as an effective securement of release by price and by power to construe it as anything less than the effectual accomplishment which secures the salvation of those who are its objects. Christ did not come to put men in a redeemable position but to redeem to himself a people.' (John Murray, *Redemption Accomplished and Applied*, p. 63)

*V*13: **For if the blood of bulls and of goats, and the ashes of an heifer sprinkling the unclean, sanctifieth to the purifying of the flesh:**

Nevertheless the blood sacrifices which were offered by the priests of the tabernacle did serve to purify the flesh from ceremonial uncleanness. The defilement produced by physical contact with a dead body excluded the person affected from the congregation of Israel, but the sprinkling of the ashes of an heifer provided a ritual cleansing which again fitted him to join in the worship of God. [*Num* 19] 'The spiritual Israelite derived, in these legal rites, spiritual blessings not flowing from them, but from the Antitype. Ceremonial sacrifices released from *temporal penalties* and *ceremonial disqualifications*: Christ's sacrifice releases from *everlasting penalties* (*v* 12) and *moral impurities of conscience* disqualifying from access to God (*v* 14).' (A. R. Fausset)

*V*14: **How much more shall the blood of Christ, who through the eternal Spirit offered himself without spot to God, purge your conscience from dead works to serve the living God?**

If therefore even the blood of animals sufficed to secure such an external purification, how much more shall the blood of Christ effect the moral cleansing of the conscience?

**who through the eternal Spirit** 'This does not refer to the Holy Spirit, but to the Spirit which was His own, that is, to *Christ's divine nature.* Also, the word *eternal* here means *heavenly.* Therefore the meaning is that *through the heavenly aspect of His deity* Christ makes the offering. This is also borne out by the opening words of the Epistle: ". . . the Son, after he had made propitiation of sins in himself." The verb here is in the middle voice, which is significant, indicating something taking place *within Christ's Person.*' (G. Vos)

**offered himself** 'It was the living God manifested in flesh who was both our High Priest and victim; and He stamped His own glory on the propitiation for our sins, both on the priestly act and on the ransom offered.' (John Brown)

**without spot to God** The efficacy of the Levitical offerings depended upon the outward perfection of the sacrifice, but what Christ offered to God was *Himself,* an offering without inward blemish or moral impurity of any kind. [1 *Pet* 1:19]

**cleanse your conscience from dead works to serve the living God?** (RV) 'We must note the aim of atonement which is *to serve the living God.* We are not cleansed by Christ so that we can immerse ourselves continually in fresh dirt, but in order that our purity may serve the glory of God. He goes on to say that nothing can proceed from us which is pleasing to God until we are cleansed by the blood of Christ. Since we are all enemies of God before our reconciliation, all that we do is likewise hateful to Him. The beginning of true worship is therefore reconciliation. Because no work is so pure or free from sin as to be pleasing to God by itself, cleansing by the blood of Christ which destroys all stains must necessarily intervene. This is the true contrast between the living God and dead works.' (Calvin)

*V15:* **And for this cause he is the mediator of the new testament, that by means of death, for the redemption of the transgressions that were under the first testament, they which are called might receive the promise of eternal inheritance.**

It is on account of the infinite superiority of His sacrifice that Christ is the Mediator of the 'new covenant' (RV), for though the old covenant extended a promise of eternal life it was unable to confer it because the blood of animals could never provide a real atonement for sin. As the death of Christ was therefore indispensably necessary in order to cancel the guilt of those who were called in the former dispensation, the present readers had no reason to be offended by it since all who receive the 'eternal' inheritance do so in virtue of that 'eternal' redemption which was obtained by means of His 'eternal' spirit. (*vv* 12, 14, 15) (Lenski) 'His death, as is here stated, was an expiation for moral transgressions under the first covenant, and which had remained unexpiated, though remitted in the forbearance of God [*Rom* 3:25]. On the ground of the previous proof as to the efficacy of Christ's sacrifice, the apostle declares that it was retrospective, and atoned for transgressions till then unexpiated. Christ's atonement cannot be conceived of except as a proper expiation, if we trace these two elements: it took the place of the Old Testament sacrifices, which were undoubtedly atonements in their own sphere; and it accomplished what they, from their insufficiency, could not accomplish.' (Smeaton)

*V16:* **For where a testament is, there must also of necessity be the death of the testator.**

*V*17: **For a testament is of force after men are dead: otherwise it is of no strength at all while the testator liveth.**

'There is no more possibility or feasibility of interference with the effective application of the blessings of the covenant than there is of interfering with a testamentary disponement once the testator has died. This use of the testamentary provision of Roman law to illustrate the inviolable security accruing from the sacrificial death of Christ serves to underline the unilateral character of the new covenant. One thing is apparent, that a testament is a unilateral disposition of possession. How totally foreign to the notion of compact, contract, or agreement is the disposition or dispensation which can be illustrated in respect of its effective operation by a last will!' (John Murray, *The Covenant of Grace*, p. 30)

*V*18: **Whereupon neither the first testament was dedicated without blood.**

In this verse the reference to the blood of sacrifice shows that the author reverts to the concept of a 'covenant.' (RV) Those who were tempted to look askance at the blood of Christ are here reminded that the Sinaitic covenant was not inaugurated without the shedding of blood. [*Exod* 24:3–8]

*V*19: **For when Moses had spoken every precept to all the people according to the law, he took the blood of calves and of goats, with water, and scarlet wool, and hyssop, and sprinkled both the book, and all the people,**

*V*20: **Saying, This is the blood of the testament which God hath enjoined unto you.**

Several details in this description are not found in the Exodus narrative but though the sources used by the author are no longer available for our scrutiny we are not thereby obliged to doubt the accuracy of his inspired account of the matter. [2 *Tim* 3:16] What he wishes to emphasize is that all the provisions of that covenant were solemnly ratified by Moses when he sprinkled both the book and the people with the blood which he then identified as 'the blood of the covenant.' (RV)

**V21: Moreover he sprinkled with blood both the tabernacle, and all the vessels of the ministry.**

Subsequently even the tabernacle itself and all its sacred appurtenances required to be cleansed by blood so that they might be used by sinners without becoming defiled. (Lenski) [*Lev* 16:14–20]

**V22: And almost all things are by the law purged with blood; and without shedding of blood is no remission.**

In fact under the law 'I may almost say, all things are cleansed with blood' (RV), without which 'there is no remission.' Although those who could only afford a bloodless offering still obtained remission, such exceptions nevertheless derived their efficacy from the universal rule on which they were based. [*Lev* 5:11–13] The author's insistence upon this principle makes it hard to see how there can be any remission of sins granted through the 'unbloody' offering of the mass. 'There is in the mass no real Christ, no suffering, and no bleeding. And a bloodless sacrifice is ineffectual. The writer of the book of Hebrews says that "apart from shedding of blood there is no remission" of sin [9:22]; and John says, "The blood of Jesus his Son cleanseth us from all sin" [1 *John* 1:7]. Since admittedly there is no blood in the mass, it simply cannot be a sacrifice for sin.' (L. Boettner, *Roman Catholicism*, p. 227) This is therefore an unscriptural practice which 'dishonours and degrades the one perfect and all-sufficient sacrifice of Christ, by representing it as repeated, or rather caricatured, daily and hourly by the juggling mummery of a priest.' (William Cunningham, *Historical Theology*, Vol. II, p. 143)

*V*23 : **It was therefore necessary that the patterns of things in the heavens should be purified with these; but the heavenly things themselves with better sacrifices than these.**

'The earthly tabernacle, as God's dwelling, might have been supposed to be hallowed by His presence and to need no cleansing, but being also His meeting-place with men it required to be cleansed. And so our heavenly relations with God, and all wherewith we seek to approach Him, need cleansing. In themselves things heavenly need no cleansing, but as entered upon by sinful men they need it. Our eternal relations with God require purification.' (*Expositor's Greek Testament*, quoted by K. Wuest)

**better sacrifices** Here the plural is put for the singular 'because he had used the plural when speaking of the purification of the earthly tabernacle, and because of the superiority of Christ's sacrifice, which exceeded all other sacrifices in its power and efficacy.' (Kuinoel, cited by Brown)

*V*24: **For Christ is not entered into the holy places made with hands, which are the figures of the true; but into heaven itself, now to appear in the presence of God for us:**

Christ therefore has not entered a holy place made with hands which was but a copy of the celestial reality, but has appeared in heaven itself as the representative of a people who now enjoy through Him continuous and unrestricted access into the very presence of God.

but into heaven itself, now to appear before the face of God for us: (RV) 'It is enough that Jesus *shows Himself for us* to the Father: the sight satisfies God in our behalf. He brings before the face of God no offering which, as only sufficing for a time, needs renewal; but He is in person, by the eternal Spirit in Him, our eternally-present offering before God.' (A. R. Fausset)

*V25*: **Nor yet that he should offer himself often, as the high priest entereth into the holy place every year with blood of others;**

Unlike the High Priest who entered the holy place each year 'with blood not his own' (RV), Christ made the unrepeatable offering of His own blood through which He entered into the heavenly sanctuary once for all.

*V26*: **For then must he often have suffered since the foundation of the world: but now once in the end of the world hath he appeared to put away sin by the sacrifice of himself.**

**For then must he often have suffered since the foundation of the world:** The sufficiency of this offering is proved by its finality, for if its benefits did not extend to former generations, then He must have suffered continually from the time that man first became a sinner. But since He did not so suffer, it is evident that His offering needs no supplement. Furthermore, the author shows that he makes no distinction between Christ's death and His entrance into the sanctuary by thus defining His offering in terms of His suffering. For *He* did not painlessly present the blood of others but offered *Himself*, and this entailed mortal suffering which clearly cannot be repeated. 'I ask you to observe that in the Epistle to the Hebrews not only is the sacrifice set before us as *one*, but the *offering* or *oblation* is *once*, and *once for all*. Moreover, the date of this *once* is (as it seems to me, at least) most clearly fixed. It belongs to the Cross, and to the Cross alone. It is identified with the passion; so that a second *offering* would require a second dying, and a continuous oblation could not be without a continuous victim state of sacrificial suffering.' (N. Dimock, cited by Hammond)

**but now once at the consummation of the ages** (RV margin) 'Jewish thought tended to divide time into the present (evil) age and the (blessed) age to come. It is the conviction of our writer, as of the New Testament writers generally, that that blessed age had come, and that the Christians were receiving the benefits.' (R. V. G. Tasker) [1 *Cor* 10:11]

**hath he been manifested to put away sin by the sacrifice of himself.** (RV) But now that Christ has been historically manifested on earth He has annulled sin's power by exhausting its penalty in His priestly self-offering upon the Cross. [2 *Cor* 5:21]

*V*27: **And as it is appointed unto men once to die, but after this the judgment:**

*V*28: **So Christ was once offered to bear the sins of many; and unto them that look for him shall he appear the second time without sin unto salvation.**

Death became a divine appointment for man through his one primal act of disobedience, and the judgment which must follow it registers the unfavourable verdict of God upon a sinful life. Such a verdict could only be reversed through a vicarious satisfaction for sin, and this Christ accomplished in accordance with the prophecy of Isaiah. (*Is* 53:12: 'to bear the sins of many.') The dreadful anguish with which Cardinal Newman's

[116]

Gerontius faced the Great Assize is in startling contrast to the teaching of the New Testament which speaks of the believer's 'boldness in the day of judgment.' [1 *John* 4:17] Plainly this is not a presumptuous confidence, for the assurance of his complete absolution from all guilt is based upon the full satisfaction which Christ made for his sin. It is to be further noted that the extent of the atonement is determined by the number who are finally saved by it. The passage represents the second advent of Christ, this time without even the imputation of sin, as the climacteric event which will consummate the salvation of 'the many' for whom He once suffered.

**shall appear a second time, apart from sin, to them that wait for him, unto salvation.** (RV) 'It is the great exercise of faith, to live on the invisible actings of Christ on the behalf of the church. So also the foundation of it doth consist in our infallible expectation of his second appearance, of our seeing him again, *Acts* 1:11. . . . The present long-continued absence of Christ in heaven is the great trial of the world. God doth give the world *a trial by faith in Christ*, as he gave it *a trial by obedience in Adam*. Faith is tried by difficulties. When Christ did appear, it was under such circumstances as turned all unbelievers from him. His state was then a state of infirmity, reproach, and suffering. He appeared in the flesh. Now he is in glory, he appeareth not. As many refused him when he appeared, because it was in outward weakness; so many refuse him now he is in glory, because he appeareth not. Faith alone can conflict with and conquer these difficulties.' (John Owen) [*Rev* 22:20]

# CHAPTER TEN

*V*1: **For the law having a shadow of good things to come, and not the very image of the things, can never with those sacrifices which they offered year by year continually make the comers thereunto perfect.**

Having proved the finality of Christ's sacrifice, the author next insists upon its perfection. He begins by conceding that the law had indeed a shadow of the good things to come, but a shadow could never fulfil the expectations to which it gave rise. However, at last this unsubstantial promise had given place to the very image itself, for the new age which was inaugurated by the finished work of Christ 'is not merely a reproduction of the Heavenly Reality, but its actual substance, the Reality itself come down from heaven.' (G. Vos) Thus the law could never make perfect those who sought to draw near to God through the continuous succession of sacrifices which it prescribed, and this was because 'no repetition of the shadow can amount to the substance.' (A. B. Davidson)

*V*2: **For then would they not have ceased to be offered? because that the worshippers once purged should have had no more conscience of sins.**

The question summons the readers to reflect on the significance of these repeated offerings, for if any one of them had been adequate to pacify the consciences of the worshippers by effecting a real purification of sins then this would have brought the series to an end. The argument used here suggests that the Epistle was written before A.D. 70 when the destruction of the temple ensured the cessation of all sacrifices. 'All peace with God is resolved into a purging atonement made for sin: "Being once purged."' (John Owen) [*John* 13:10 RV]

### *V3*: But in those sacrifices there is a remembrance again made of sins every year.

'It would not have occurred to an observant Jew under the Mosaic covenant to say that the Day of Atonement involved an annual "remembrance" of sins; he would have said, rather, that there was an annual *removal* of sins. Our author might have replied, truly enough, that the ritual designed to effect the removal of sins necessarily involves their remembrance; but he is influenced chiefly by the promise that under the new covenant God will remember His people's sins no more. Since the new covenant is contrasted with the old, the implication is that there was no such absolute wiping out of sins from the divine record under the sacrificial law.' (F. F. Bruce)

### *V4*: For it is not possible that the blood of bulls and of goats should take away sins.

He does not deal here with the positive value of what had been a divine appointment, but only shows what these sacrifices could not do when considered in themselves. This judgment was timely, for to forsake Christ in order to return to a system of worship that had outlived its usefulness, would amount to a rejection of the only real sacrifice in favour of the blood of beasts which could never take away the sin of man.

### *V5*: Wherefore when he cometh into the world, he saith, Sacrifice and offering thou wouldest not, but a body hast thou prepared me:

*V*6: **In burnt offerings and sacrifices for sin thou hast had no pleasure.**

*V*7: **Then said I, Lo, I come (in the volume of the book it is written of me,) to do thy will, O God.**

**Wherefore when he cometh into the world, he saith,** The author sees a prophetic anticipation of the whole earthly course of Christ in the words uttered by David in *Psalm* 40: 6–8. 'It is not as if Christ and *not* David speaks; but Christ, whose spirit already dwells and works in David, and who will hereafter receive from David his human nature, now already speaks in him.' (Delitzsch, cited by Lenski)

**Sacrifice and offering thou wouldest not, but a body hast thou prepared me:** The quotation follows the Greek version of the Psalm, and Delitzsch also suggests that its substitution of 'a body hast thou prepared me' for the Hebrew 'mine ears hast thou digged' (AV margin) was due to the desire of the translators to make it more intelligible to Greek readers. (cf. Lenski) In either case, there is no material difference in meaning, for attentive hearing prepares for obedient service. [*Is* 50:4–7] And it was Christ's voluntary submission to the will of God which distinguished the offering of His body from the forced and non-rational offering of the bodies of beasts in sacrifice.

**In burnt offerings and sacrifices for sin thou hast had no pleasure.** God was well pleased with such sacrifices 'in so far as they were in obedience to His positive Old Testament command, but *not as having intrinsic efficacy to atone for sin*, such as Christ's sacrifice had. Contrast *Matt* 3:17.' (A. R. Fausset)

**Then said I, Lo, I am come (In the roll of the book it is written of me) To do thy will, O God.** (RV) 'There is nothing of irresponsibility or adventure in Christ's life and death. It is all obedience, and therefore it is all revelation. We see God in it because it is not His own will but the will of the Father which it accomplished. Even when we come to consider its relation to sin, this must be borne in mind. Atonement is not something contrived, as it were, behind the Father's back; it is the Father's way of making it possible for the sinful to have fellowship with Him.' (James Denney, *The Death of Christ*, p. 122)

*V*8: **Above when he said, Sacrifice and offering and burnt offerings and offering for sin thou wouldest not, neither hadst pleasure therein; which are offered by the law;**

*V*9: **Then said he, Lo, I come to do thy will, O God. He taketh away the first, that he may establish the second.**

These words of the Messiah therefore show that God's dissatisfaction with the sacrifices which were offered according to law pointed forward to their replacement by His own perfect obedience to the divine will. Hence the abrogation of the first must mean the establishment of the second.

*V*10: **By the which will we are sanctified through the offering of the body of Jesus Christ once for all.**

**By which will we have been sanctified through the offering of the body of Jesus Christ** (RV) 'The will of God, with which we are here concerned, is not satisfied by an obedience which comes short of death. For it is not merely the preceptive will of God, His will that men should do right and live according to His holy law, which Christ came to fulfil; it is His gracious will, a will which has as its aim that sinful men should be constituted into a people for Himself, a will which has resolved that their sin should be so dealt with as no longer to keep them at a distance from Him; a will, in short, that sinners should find a standing in His sight. And in that will we are sanctified, not merely by Christ's fulfilment of the law of God as it is binding on man in general, but by His fulfilment of the law as it is binding on sinful men, by His obedient suffering of death as that in which God's mind in relation to sin finds its final expression.' (James Denney)

**once for all.** That which has been completed *for* the believer obviously cannot refer to a gradual process *within* the believer. Accordingly, this 'sanctification' is the objective achievement of Christ which has secured the purification of His people and forever set them apart for the service of God. It has a forensic import which is analogous to the Pauline concept of 'justification.'

*V*11: **And every priest standeth daily ministering and offering oftentimes the same sacrifices, which can never take away sins:**

*V*12: **But this man, after he had offered one sacrifice for sins for ever, sat down on the right hand of God;**

The Levitical priests must stand as they daily offer the very same sacrifices which can never take away the guilt of sins, but *this* Priest after He had offered one sacrifice for sins for ever, then took his seat 'on the right hand of the Majesty on high.' [*Heb* 1:3] Christ's heavenly enthronement bears witness to the eternal validity of that one historic sacrifice by which He made reconciliation for iniquity and brought in everlasting righteousness. [*Dan* 9:24]

*V*13: **From henceforth expecting till his enemies be made his footstool.**

The author's intention in thus completing the substance of *Ps* 110:1 is probably to warn the readers 'not to let themselves be numbered among the enemies of the exalted Christ, but rather to be reckoned as His friends and companions by preserving their fidelity to the end.' (F. F. Bruce) [*Heb* 3:14; 10: 26–31]

*V*14: **For by one offering he hath perfected for ever them that are sanctified.**

This verse rules out the possibility of any further offering for sins either on earth or in heaven for it affirms that Christ has perfected for ever those who are consecrated to God by His *one* offering on their behalf. According to John Flavel this means, '*That the oblation made unto God by Jesus Christ, is of unspeakable value, and everlasting efficacy, to perfect all them that are, or shall be sanctified, to the end of the world.*' (*Works*, Vol. I, p. 155)

*V*15: **Whereof the Holy Ghost also is a witness to us: for after that he had said before,**

*V*16: **This is the covenant that I will make with them after those days, saith the Lord, I will put my laws into their hearts, and in their minds will I write them;**

*V*17: **And their sins and iniquities will I remember no more.**

*V*18: **Now where remission of these is, there is no more offering for sin.**

Earlier in the Epistle the author had drawn the attention of his readers to the newness of that covenant which had made the first old, but here he appeals once more to this testimony of the Holy Spirit in order to emphasize its finality. [*Jer* 31:31 f.; *Heb* 8:8 f.] God's promise to remember the sins of His people no more is the outstanding feature of the new covenant, for the continual remembrance of sins under the old economy showed the insufficiency of its constant sacrifices to atone for sin. But Christ blotted out the sins of His people beyond recall when He offered himself to God on their behalf. His death ratified the new covenant and abolished the old order. Thus where there is the full remission of sins, no possibility of any further offering for sin remains.

*V*19: **Having therefore, brethren, boldness to enter into the holiest by the blood of Jesus,**

Exposition now gives place to exhortation, and the remainder of the Epistle is devoted to a detailed application of the eloquent appeal which begins in this verse and extends to *v* 25. The author addresses his readers as 'brethren' to remind them of those privileges which are inseparable from their profession of faith in Christ, for it is as those who realize that their acceptance by God rests entirely upon the sacrificial death of their great High Priest that he bids them boldly to enter the heavenly sanctuary. 'Christians do not enter the holiest *with* the blood of Jesus, for then they would be priests, anew opening up the way, whenever they approached, by a new offering; the view of the passage is that the way is opened up once for all by the offering of the Son [9:12, 28; 10:12], and lies for ever open because He abides before the face of God for us [9:24]; and it is on this fact, called here the blood of Jesus, that the glad confidence of believers in regard to entrance is based.' (A. B. Davidson)

*V*20: **By a new and living way, which he hath consecrated for us, through the veil, that is to say, his flesh;**

'**which.** The antecedent is "the entering;" not, as the English version, "way." Translate, "which (entering) He has consecrated (not as though already existing, but *has* INAUGURATED *as a new thing* [ENEKAINISEN]: note, *ch* 9:18) for us (as) a new [PROSPHATON, *recent*: recently opened, *Rom* 16: 25, 26] and living way" (not the lifeless way through the law offering of blood of *dead* victims, but *vital*, and of perpetual

efficacy, because the *living* and *life-giving* Saviour is that *way*.)'
(A. R. Fausset) [*John* 14:6]

**through the veil, that is to say, his flesh;** As there was no
way into the inner sanctuary of the tabernacle except through
the veil, so the flesh of Jesus affords the only means of access to
the heavenly sanctuary. 'The crucified Christ is the entrance,
the entrance veil. "No man cometh to the Father but *by me*,"
*John* 14:6, by my blood, by my flesh, by this veil. This veil
shuts out and forever hides the Father from all those who
spurn it as the means of entry.' (Lenski) [cf. *Matt* 27:51]

*V*21: **And having an high priest over the house of God;**

**And having a great priest over the house of God;** (RV)
This further reminder of the greatness of the Priest who now
presides over the house of God is designed to encourage
their confident approach to the throne of grace, and also to
warn them against any return to the ministrations of a discarded priesthood. 'Christ could not be a high priest unless the
former priests were divested of their office, since theirs was a
different order. He means therefore that all those things which
Christ changed at His coming are to be let go. He sets Him
over the whole house of God so that whoever wishes to have
a place in the Church must submit to Christ and choose Him
and no other as his leader and ruler.' (Calvin) [*Heb* 3:1–6; 4:
14–16]

*V*22: **Let us draw near with a true heart in full assurance
of faith, having our hearts sprinkled from an evil conscience, and our bodies washed with pure water.**

It is in virtue of the sufficiency of Christ's one offering for sin
and the perfection of His priesthood that they are exhorted to
draw near to God in worship, but because 'to approach God
was a priestly prerogative under the old order, the author

describes the Christian access to God in sacerdotal metaphors.' (T. Hewitt) ('Let us draw near . . .' is explained in the comment on *ch* 4:16) The verse is a clear denial of an *ex opere operato* conception of grace, for the use of such ritual language shows that the code which called for the meticulous preparation of the body for worship must find its spiritual parallel in the individual Christian's consciousness.

**with a true heart** Sincerity is the prime requisite in every approach to the God who requires 'truth in the inward parts,' and who hates all hypocrisy, falsehood, and deceit. [*Ps* 51:6; *John* 4:24]

**in full assurance of faith,** This 'respects not the assurance that any have of their own salvation, nor any degree of such an assurance; it is only the full satisfaction of our souls and consciences in the reality and efficacy of the priesthood of Christ to give us acceptance with God, in opposition unto all other ways and means thereof, that is intended.' (John Owen)

**having our hearts sprinkled from an evil conscience,** As the ritual purity of the Levitical priests was secured by the sprinkling of sacrificial blood, so the Christian is cleansed from an evil conscience by faith in the blood of Christ. [*Exod* 29:21; *Heb* 9:14] 'Daily do we need to confess our sins, that we may be daily pardoned and "cleansed from all unrighteousness" [1 *John* 1:9]. An uneasy conscience is as real a barrier to fellowship with Jehovah, as ceremonial defilement was to a Jew.' (Arthur Pink)

**and our bodies washed with pure water.** This washing is to be no more literally understood than is the application of the blood of Christ to the conscience. It has no reference to Christian Baptism, but rather alludes to the cleansing of the priests under the law. [*Exod* 29:4; 30:19–21] 'Whereas the sprinkling of the heart from an evil conscience respects the *internal* and unknown sins of the mind; so this of washing the body doth the sins that are outwardly acted and perpetrated. And the body is said to be washed from them, *1st*. Because they are outward, in opposition unto those that are only inherent, in the mind. *2dly*. Because the body is the instrument of the perpetration of them; hence are they called "deeds of the body;" the "members of the body;" our "earthly members," *Rom* 3:13–15; 8:13, *Col* 3:3–5. *3dly*. Because the body is defiled by them, by some of them in an especial manner, 1 *Cor* 6. Pure water, wherewith the body is to be washed, is that which is promised, *Ezek* 36:25, 26; – the assistance of the sanctifying Spirit, by virtue of the sacrifice of Christ.' (John Owen)

*V23*: **Let us hold fast the profession of our faith without wavering; (for he is faithful that promised;)**

**Let us hold fast the confession of our hope that it waver not; for he is faithful that promised:** (RV) Since the author knows that their confidence in the promise is best nourished by a firm conviction of the reliability of the Promiser, he reinforces this call to continue in the faith by reminding them that the attainment of the hope they had confessed is based on the unchanging faithfulness of God. [1 *Cor* 1:9; 1 *Thess* 5:24; *Heb* 11:11] Perseverance is the hall mark of a genuine interest in Christ, but inconstancy imperils the eternal inheritance, for the hope of salvation always withers when the frank confession of it wavers.

*V24*: **And let us consider one another to provoke unto love and to good works:**

In place of the selfish individualism which only fosters strife, they must constantly seek to encourage and edify one another by those deeds of love which will express the reality of their fellowship in Christ. The professing Church today sorely stands in need of a renewal of such 'provocations' ! [*Phil* 2:1–5]

*V25*: **Not forsaking the assembling of ourselves together, as the manner of some is; but exhorting one another: and so much the more, as ye see the day approaching.**

It is because the New Testament knows nothing of a solitary Christianity that the author presses upon his readers the duty of assembling together for worship, instruction, and mutual encouragement. Even if it is not welcome, this warning is nevertheless necessary for their spiritual welfare, as the partial neglect of the means of grace is the first step towards a total decline from grace. Indeed the sluggishness of some should rather serve to quicken them to greater diligence in the encouragement of one another, and all the more so as they see 'the day approaching.' The Early Church did not consider the second advent of Christ to be an interesting topic for cold chronological calculation for it lived in the earnest expectation of the imminence of this great event. [*Rev* 22:20] 'The Church being in all ages uncertain how soon Christ is coming, *the day* is, in each age, practically always near; whence believers are called on always to be watching for it as nigh at hand. The Hebrews were now living close upon one great type and foretaste of it – the destruction of Jerusalem [*Matt* 24].' (A. R. Fausset)

*V26*: **For if we sin wilfully after that we have received the knowledge of the truth, there remaineth no more sacrifice for sins.**

In order that they might realize the consequences of severing their connection with Christ by a permanent withdrawal from the Christian assembly, the writer describes the awful doom which awaits those who are found to be apostates on the day of judgment. It is a dreadful disclosure of the fate which must inevitably overtake anyone who, after having professed an interest in Christ's salvation, then deliberately and persistently repudiates it. This settled *state* of rebellion against the gospel is not to be confused with isolated *acts* of sin which may be committed through weakness or ignorance. In *ch* 6: 4–6 'the warning was, that if there be not diligence in *progressing*, a falling off, and then an apostasy, will ensue: here it is, if there be lukewarmness in Christian *communion*, apostasy ensues.' (A. R. Fausset)

**there remaineth no more sacrifice for sins,** 'The apostate must perish, not because the sacrifice of Christ is not of efficacy enough to expiate even his guilt, but because, continuing in his apostasy, he will have nothing to do with that sacrifice which is the only available sacrifice for sin.' (John Brown)

*V*27: **But a certain fearful looking for of judgment and fiery indignation, which shall devour the adversaries.**

Having spurned the sacrifice of Christ, there remains for the apostate only a fearful expectation of the furious fire of divine judgment which is to devour the adversaries. [*Heb* 12:29; *Rev* 21:8] The word 'certain' indicates a punishment of 'undefined, undefinable magnitude – something that is inexpressible, inconceivable ... The most dreadful conception comes infinitely short of the more dreadful reality. We can only say of it, "It is a certain fearful punishment which the apostate has to expect."' (John Brown)

*V*28: **He that despised Moses' law died without mercy under two or three witnesses:**

*V*29: **Of how much sorer punishment, suppose ye, shall he be thought worthy, who hath trodden under foot the Son of God, and hath counted the blood of the covenant, wherewith he was sanctified, an unholy thing, and hath done despite unto the Spirit of grace?**

The equity of the judgment is vindicated by the enormity of the offence, for if the person who set at nought the law of Moses was punished without mercy, then it is evident that he who is guilty of despising the Son must be visited with far greater severity. [*Deut* 17:2–7] This sin is unpardonable because a contemptuous rejection of the gospel is nothing less than a trampling under foot of the Son of God, a profanation of the blood of the new covenant, and a scorning of the Spirit of grace.

**the blood . . . wherewith he was sanctified** Although the apostate never was regenerate he was once externally dedicated to God by a profession of faith in Christ's atoning blood, and it was from this alone that he fell away.

*V*30: **For we know him that hath said, Vengeance belongeth unto me, I will recompense, saith the Lord. And again, The Lord shall judge his people.**

**For we know him that hath said,** The author now appeals to their own knowledge of the absolute rectitude of the Judge as he introduces two quotations which confirm the righteousness of the sentence which is to be executed upon all such despisers of the gospel. 'It is a most profitable exercise for the soul to be often engaged in contemplating the Divine attributes, pondering God's almighty power, ineffable holiness, unimpeachable veracity, exact justice, absolute faithfulness and terrible severity. Christ Himself has bidden us "Fear Him which is able to destroy both soul and body in hell" [*Matt* 10: 28]. The better God's character be known, the more we heed that exhortation of Christ's, the clearer shall we perceive that there is nothing unsuited to the holiness of God in what Scripture affirms concerning His dealings with the wicked. It is because the true nature of sin is so little viewed in the light of God's awful holiness, that so many fail to recognize its *infinite* demerits.' (Arthur Pink)

**Vengeance belongeth unto me, I will recompense, saith the Lord.** Both quotations are from the Song of Moses. The first, *Deut* 32:35, appears in the version followed by Paul in *Rom* 12:19. Although in their original setting these words refer to the vengeance which will overtake the enemies of Israel, they state a principle of universal application, for as Trapp tersely remarks, 'if God will avenge his elect, *Luke* 18: 7, how much more his Son and his Spirit!'

**And again, The Lord shall judge his people.** '– in grace, or else anger, as each deserves: here "judge" so as to punish the reprobate; there [*Deut* 32:35, 36], "judge" so as to interpose in behalf of His people.' (A. R. Fausset)

*V*31: **It is a fearful thing to fall into the hands of the living God.**

The dumb idols of the heathen could neither help nor punish their self-deceived devotees, but because Israel's God *lives* He has the power to fulfil every promise and to make His threatened judgments a frightful reality. Thus 'it is a fearful thing to fall into the hands of the living God,' for, says Calvin, 'mortal man, however inimical he may be, cannot carry his enmity beyond death, but the power of God is not confined to such narrow limits. We often escape from men, we cannot escape the judgment of God.'

*V*32: **But call to remembrance the former days, in which, after ye were illuminated, ye endured a great fight of afflictions;**

As with the earlier warning, so this is followed by words of encouragement. (cf. *ch* 6:9 f.) Here the author bids them recall a particular occasion, soon after their 'enlightenment' (RV), when their faith had emerged unscathed from a great contest of sufferings. Although this persecution was severe it appears from *ch* 12:4 that no Christian lives were lost, and this would rule out Jerusalem as the scene of their trial. W. Manson suggests that the Epistle was written to Jewish Christians in Rome shortly before Nero's bloodbath (A.D. 64), and that these verses (10:32-34) refer to their experiences during A.D. 49 when the Emperor Claudius ordered all Jews to leave the city because, according to Suetonius, 'they were constantly indulging in riots at the instigation of Chrestus.' (cited by F. F. Bruce) [cf. *Acts* 18:2] 'If we assume that the name "Chrestus" here is a garbled form of Christus, the meaning will be that Messianic agitations breaking out among the Jews at Rome had drawn down upon them the unfavourable notice of the public authorities, the guardians of the peace, and Claudius acted accordingly. . . . The most plausible explanation of the whole episode is that Christian propaganda had been introduced into the synagogues at Rome and had created considerable ferment.' (W. Manson, *The Epistle to the Hebrews*, p. 41)

*V*33: **Partly, whilst ye were made a gazingstock both by reproaches and afflictions; and partly, whilst ye became companions of them that were so used.**

'In two ways the Hebrews, just after their conversion, had endured such sufferings – partly in being themselves subjected publicly to reproaches and sufferings, and partly in becoming voluntary sympathizers and sharers with them who were so used, or whose Christian life was led under such troubles.' (A. B. Davidson)

*V*34: **For ye had compassion of me in my bonds, and took joyfully the spoiling of your goods, knowing in yourselves that ye have in heaven a better and an enduring substance.**

**For ye both had compassion on them that were in bonds,** (RV) Despite the personal risk involved, they did not shrink from visiting those of their brethren who were imprisoned for the sake of the gospel, and willingly ministered to their needs.

**and took joyfully the spoiling of your possessions, knowing that ye yourselves have a better possession and an abiding one.** (RV) It was because they knew that they had a better eternal inheritance that they were enabled to meet the loss of their worldly goods with joyful fortitude. 'This will make a rich amends for all they can lose and suffer here. In heaven they shall have a better life, a better estate, better liberty, better society, better hearts, better work, every thing better.' (Matthew Henry) [*Matt* 6:19–21; 1 *Pet* 1:4]

*V*35: **Cast not away therefore your confidence, which hath great recompence of reward.**

Since you endured so much in 'former days' (*v* 32) do not now cast away your 'boldness' (RV) which has 'great recompence of reward.' This is 'of a kind which no mercenary self-seeker would seek: holiness will be its own reward; self-devotion for Christ will be its own rich recompence.' (A. R. Fausset) [*Gen* 15:1; *Matt* 5:12; 10:32]

*V*36: **For ye have need of patience, that, after ye have done the will of God, ye might receive the promise.**

If they are to receive the promised salvation they have need of patience both to do and to bear the will of God. For it is only the recognition that the will of God includes the afflictions that accompany a profession of faith in Christ which enables the believer to sustain them. [1 *Pet* 4:19]

[133]

**ye might receive the promise.** 'The consideration of eternal life as the free effect of the grace of God and Christ, and as proposed in a gracious promise, is a thousand times more full of spiritual refreshment unto a believer, than if he should conceive of it or look upon it merely as a reward proposed unto our own doings or merits.' (John Owen)

*V*37: **For yet a little while, and he that shall come will come, and will not tarry.**

*V*38: **Now the just shall live by faith: but if any man draw back, my soul shall have no pleasure in him.**

The author, writing under the direct inspiration of the Holy Spirit, here freely adapts this quotation from the Greek version of the Old Testament, thus giving his readers the authoritative interpretation of the prophet's message. [*Hab* 2:3, 4] 'The Spirit of God guided the writers of the New Testament in their general usage and in their choice of language from the Septuagint, so that what they wrote was inspired of Him. It was inspired, however, not because it was taken from the Septuagint, but rather, because it was breathed out by Him and written down by those whom the Spirit bore as they composed the New Testament writings.' (E. J. Young, *Thy Word is Truth*, p. 147)

**For yet a very little while,** (RV) This phrase is also found in *Is* 26:20 LXX, but as the author's mind is so deeply imbued with Scripture it is unnecessary to assume that this is a conscious quotation of it. This is no time for them to abandon the faith. Let them hold fast to their original confidence, and in a very little while they will receive the promise.

**He that cometh shall come, and shall not tarry.** (RV) 'Christ will appear soon in order to bestow the promised glory. This repeats *Hab* 2:3 with a personal subject and thus only adopts some of the prophet's language to express the writer's great New Testament thought, namely our certainty of Christ's second coming. He will most certainly come; his very name is still "the coming One." He has received that name because of his first coming but also because of his second coming.' (Lenski)

**But the righteous one shall live by faith:** (RV margin) He whom God declares righteous evidences the reality of his justification by living a life of faithfulness to God. 'The apostle's purpose is to show that those who are reckoned just before God can only live by faith. The future tense of the word "live" shows the continuity of life.' (Calvin) [*Hab* 2:4 also quoted in *Rom* 1:17 and *Gal* 3:11]

**And if he shrink back, my soul hath no pleasure in him.** (RV) Yet if this same righteous man were to shrink back, then God would take no pleasure in him, for only 'he that endureth to the end shall be saved.' [*Matt* 10:22] 'Christ hath no delights in dastards, turn-coats, run-a-ways, he will not employ them so far as to break a pitcher, or bear a torch, *Judg* 7:7.' (Trapp)

*V*39: **But we are not of them who draw back unto perdition; but of them that believe to the saving of the soul.**

Thus they cannot escape from the necessity of choosing between these alternatives. They must realize that to renounce their interest in Christ is to 'draw back unto perdition.' In that event their loss would be total and final. However, their past history convinces the writer that they will not prove to be reprobates, but that they are of that number who 'believe to the saving of the soul.' And it is to inspire such perseverance that the illustrious faith of their ancestors is so splendidly recalled in the verses which now follow. [*ch* 11:1 f.]

# CHAPTER ELEVEN

*V*1: **Now faith is the substance of things hoped for, the evidence of things not seen.**

**Now faith is the assurance of things hoped for,** (RV) Faith does not give 'substance' to the things hoped for but is rather the subjective assurance of their reality. It is solely because the objects of hope have an existence quite apart from faith that faith in them is not misplaced. It is this which distinguishes saving faith from the faith of the imagination, for only those who put their trust in the promises of God are delivered from embracing a miserable delusion. 'By *faith* we are sure of eternal things that they ARE; by *hope* we are confident that WE SHALL HAVE them. Hope presupposes faith [*Rom* 8:25].' (A. R. Fausset)

**a conviction of things not seen.** (ARV) Such faith is more than a bare assent to a set of theological propositions; it is a regulative principle of life. [*Gal* 2:20] Thus it was 'by faith' in what was unseen that the elders overcame all the obstacles which were presented to them by the eye of sense. [*Heb* 11:27] 'The Spirit of God shows us hidden things, the knowledge of which cannot reach our senses. Eternal life is promised to us, but it is promised to the dead; we are told of the resurrection of the blessed, but meantime we are involved in corruption; we are declared to be just, and sin dwells within us; we hear that we are blessed, but meantime we are overwhelmed by untold miseries; we are promised an abundance of all good things, but we are often hungry and thirsty; God proclaims that He will come to us immediately, but seems to be deaf to our cries. What would happen to us if we did not rely on our hope, and if our minds did not emerge above the world out of the midst of darkness through the shining Word of God and by His Spirit?' (Calvin)

*V2*: **For by it the elders obtained a good report.**

Moreover it was in the exercise of this faith that the fathers were approved by God. 'Their ACTUAL Justification is presupposed, but their DECLARATIVE Justification is specially referred to; and this is represented as depending partly on the practical fruits of faith, by which it was proved to be alive and active, and partly on the divine testimony bearing witness to their acceptance.' (James Buchanan, *The Doctrine of Justification*, p. 251) [Heb 11:39]

*V3*: **Through faith we understand that the worlds were framed by the word of God, so that things which are seen were not made of things which do appear.**

Indeed it is faith alone which enables us to perceive that the universe was not made out of pre-existing materials but that it owes its existence to the creative word of God. [Gen 1:3; Ps 33:6, 9] 'Creation is here represented as a fact which we apprehend only by faith. By faith we understand (perceive, not comprehend) that the world was framed or fashioned by the word of God, that is, the word of God's power, the divine fiat, so that the things which are seen, the visible things of this world, were not made out of things which do appear, which are visible, and which are at least occasionally seen. According to this passage the world certainly was not made out of anything that is palpable to the senses.' (L. Berkhof) This verse therefore completes the author's description of faith by confirming that it is 'a conviction of things not seen.' (*v* 1)

*V*4: **By faith Abel offered unto God a more excellent sacrifice than Cain, by which he obtained witness that he was righteous, God testifying of his gifts: and by it he being dead yet speaketh.**

**By faith Abel offered unto God a more excellent sacrifice than Cain,** The faith of Abel must not be artificially restricted to the spirit in which he offered his sacrifice for it also includes his obedience to what must have been a divine appointment. [*Rom* 10:17] It was not by fancy, but by faith that he 'brought of the firstlings of his flock and of the fat thereof.' If Scripture does not provide us with an account of the institution of expiatory sacrifice, yet it can hardly be without significance that 'the very first recorded instance of acceptable worship in the family of Adam brings before us bleeding sacrifices, and seals them with the divine approbation. They appear in the first act of worship, *Gen* 4:3, 4. They are emphatically approved by God as soon as they appear.' (A. A. Hodge, cited by L. Berkhof) The worship of Cain was not accepted, because he wilfully ignored the consequences of the fall. His gift of 'the fruit of the ground' merely acknowledged God as the creator and sustainer of life, whereas saving faith is pre-eminently faith in the promised redemption. [*Gen* 3:15]

**by which he obtained witness that he was righteous, God testifying of his gifts:** God must have visibly signified His acceptance of Abel's offering for Cain was displeased by it. It is likely that He sent fire from heaven to consume the sacrifice. [*Gen* 15:7; *Lev* 9:24; *Judg* 6:21; 1 *Kings* 18:38; 2 *Chron* 7:1] 'Whomsoever God accepts or respects, he testifieth him to be righteous; that is, to be justified, and freely accepted with him. This Abel was by faith antecedently unto his offering. He was not made righteous, he was not justified by his sacrifice; but therein he showed his faith by his works: and God by acceptance of his works of obedience justified him, as Abraham was justified by works; namely, declaratively; he declared him so to be.' (John Owen)

**and by it he being dead yet speaketh.** Most commentators link this statement with a later allusion to Abel's blood which cried to God for vengeance. [Compare *Gen* 4:10 with *Heb* 12:24] However, Lenski confesses that he is unable to find that particular thought here. 'The writer says that, although he had been dead for millenniums, Abel (not his blood) speaks (not cries) to us (not to God), speaks in the Scripture record by means of his faith as to how in the Scriptures God gave him approving testimony on the basis of his sacrificial gifts as evidence of his faith. So far, even down to us, the voice of Abel's faith reaches despite his death. Chrysostom and others have Abel's voice urge us to like faith, a thought that is in line with the text.'

*V5*: **By faith Enoch was translated that he should not see death; and was not found, because God had translated him: for before his translation he had this testimony, that he pleased God.**

Enoch, like Elijah after him [2 *Kings* 2:11] did not taste death for God took him directly to heaven. This immediate glorification of the body is also to be shared by those who are alive at Christ's coming. [1 *Cor* 15:51, 52; 1 *Thess* 4:16, 17] 'This verse does not teach that Enoch had faith to be translated. God translated him because he lived a life in which He was pleased. It was by faith that he lived that life. The Mosaic commentary on his life is in the words "Enoch walked with God" [*Gen* 5:22].' (K. Wuest) Since Enoch was spiritually 'translated' [*Col*

[139]

1:13] long before his physical removal from the earthly scene, then those who wish to join God in heaven must first give evidence on earth of a similar transformation of heart and life. [*Rom* 12:2] 'He changed his place, but not his company, for he still walked with God, as in earth, so in heaven.' (Trapp)

**for he hath had witness borne to him that before his translation he had been well-pleasing unto God:** (ARV) The idea is not that God showed what He thought about Enoch by translating him. It is rather that the testimony of Scripture still furnishes us with a permanent record of the fact that for many years before this took place Enoch had pleased God.

*V*6: **But without faith it is impossible to please him: for he that cometh to God must believe that he is, and that he is a rewarder of them that diligently seek him.**

**And without faith it is impossible to be well-pleasing unto him:** (RV) Now Scripture affirms that Enoch pleased God, and therefore he must have been a man of faith, because without faith it is impossible to please Him at all. 'Where God hath put an impossibility upon any thing, it is in vain for men to attempt it. From the days of Cain multitudes have been designing to please God without faith, – all in vain; like them that would have built a tower whose top should reach to heaven.' (John Owen)

**for he that cometh to God must believe that he is,** 'To believe that "He is" means much more than assenting to the fact of a "First Cause" or to allow that there is a "Supreme Being"; it means to believe in the character of God *as* He has revealed Himself in His works, in His Word, and in Christ. He must be conceived of aright or otherwise we are only pursuing a phantom of our own imagination. Thus, to believe that "God is" is to exercise faith upon Him as *such* a Being as His Word declares Him to be: supreme sovereign, ineffably holy, almighty, inflexibly just, yet abounding in mercy and grace toward poor sinners through Christ.' (Arthur Pink)

**and that he is a rewarder of them that diligently seek him.** 'So God proved to be to Enoch. The reward is *God Himself* diligently "sought" and "walked with" in partial communion here, fully enjoyed hereafter. Cf. *Gen* 15:1.' (A. R. Fausset) [*Jer* 29:13; *Matt* 7:7, 8]

*V*7: **By faith Noah, being warned of God of things not seen as yet, moved with fear, prepared an ark to the saving of his house; by the which he condemned the world, and became heir of the righteousness which is by faith.**

Noah received the warning of the impending deluge with implicit faith despite every appearance to the contrary, and, filled with reverential awe, he built an ark for the saving of his family. During the 120 years of God's longsuffering the faithful witness of Noah as 'a preacher of righteousness' amounted to a divine condemnation of the universal unbelief which greeted his unwelcome message. Thus Noah's righteous conduct attested the reality of his justification, for his interest in 'the righteousness which is by faith' was proved by his unswerving fidelity to this exacting commission. [*Gen* 6:9 f.; 2 *Pet* 2:5] 'The example is the more instructive, as it naturally, and almost necessarily, brings before the mind the fearfully destructive efficiency of unbelief. The world that perished had materially the same message delivered to them as that which Noah received. Had they repented, there is no reason to doubt that the fearful infliction would not have taken place. Noah believed, and feared, and obeyed, and was saved. They dis-

CHAPTER II VERSE 8

believed, and mocked, and were disobedient, and perished.'
(John Brown)

*V*8: **By faith Abraham, when he was called to go out into a place which he should after receive for an inheritance, obeyed; and he went out, not knowing whither he went.**

**By faith Abraham, when he was called, obeyed** (RV) Abraham was by nature no different from any other child of Adam, for until he was called by the Lord he lived with his family in the heathen city of Ur where they 'served other gods.' [*Josh* 24:2; *Eph* 2:3] Although God had no plans for the conversion of that city, He did call one man out of it. Abraham obeyed an impossible demand to renounce the past, leaving home for an unspecified destination, because he had been effectually called by the grace of God. [*Gen* 12:1 f.] This call is distinguished from all other plausible pretences by the unquestioning obedience which it secures. 'Faith and obedience can never be severed; as the sun and the light, fire and heat. Therefore we read of the 'obedience of faith' [*Rom* 1:5]. Obedience is faith's daughter. Faith hath not only to do with the grace of God, but with the duty of the creature.' (Thomas Manton quoted by Pink)

**to go out unto a place which he was to receive for an inheritance;** (RV) Abraham himself looked for a better inheritance than the land of promise in which he lived as a stranger, but his posterity possessed it after him. (*vv* 9, 10) However, John Owen points out that even their tenure of it was for a limited season, and this came to an end when they murderously rejected the true Heir.

'Nor have the present Jews any more or better title unto the land of Canaan than unto any other country in the world. Nor shall their title be renewed thereunto upon their conversion to God. For the limitation of their right was unto that time wherein it was typical of the heavenly inheritance: that now ceasing for ever, there can be no especial title unto it revived.'

**and he went out, not knowing whither he went.** If Abraham knew not whither he went, yet he knew who had called him, and that was enough. 'Abraham winked, as it were, and put his hand into God's, to be led whithersoever he pleased.' (Trapp) In the same way the readers are to abandon the visible shadows of Judaism in favour of the invisible substance of Christianity. [2 *Cor* 4:18] 'Nothing but the faith of the Gospel can induce a man to abandon the world and commence a pilgrimage towards heaven. And wherever there is the faith of the Gospel, there will be the commencement and the prosecution of such a pilgrimage. If Abraham had continued in Mesopotamia, or stopped short of Canaan, it would have been a proof that he did not believe the divine testimony; and whatever men may profess, if they continue to love the world, and become "weary in well-doing," it is clear evidence that they have not believed the Gospel.' (John Brown) [2 *Tim* 4:10]

*V*9: **By faith he sojourned in the land of promise, as in a strange country, dwelling in tabernacles with Isaac and Jacob, the heirs with him of the same promise:**

Moreover faith enabled Abraham, as it did Isaac and Jacob after him, to live as self-confessed aliens in the land of promise, 'dwelling in tents' (RV), without so much as a square foot to call their own, except for the purchase of a burial place for Sarah. [*Gen* 23; *Acts* 7:5] 'The tent-life of the patriarchs demonstrated their pilgrim character: it made manifest their contentment to live upon the *surface* of the earth, for a tent has no foundation, and can be pitched or struck at short notice. They were sojourners here and just passing through this

[143]

wilderness-scene without striking their roots into it.' (Arthur
Pink) He whose heart is fixed upon things above holds but
loosely to the things of earth. [Col 3:1, 2] 'A little in the world
will content a Christian for his passage, but all the world, and
ten thousand times more, will not content a Christian for his
portion.' (Jeremiah Burroughs, *The Rare Jewel of Christian
Contentment*, p. 43) [*Phil* 4:11; 1 *Tim* 6:8; *Heb* 13:5]

*V*10: **For he looked for a city which hath foundations,
whose builder and maker is God.**

Abraham was content with his earthly lot because he looked
for that city with unshakeable foundations 'whose architect
and maker is God.' (RV margin) [cf. *Heb* 12:28] 'Whatever is
built by men reflects its creators in its impermanence, just as
the eternity of heavenly life fits the nature of God as its
Creator.' (Calvin)

*V*11: **Through faith also Sara herself received strength
to conceive seed, and was delivered of a child when she
was past age, because she judged him faithful who had
promised.**

**By faith even Sarah herself received power to conceive
seed when she was past age, since she counted him faithful who had promised:** (RV) 'At first she laughed, through
unbelief, at the unlikelihood; but afterward she bethought
herself, and believed. This latter is recorded, the former
pardoned. So *Gen* 18:12, "Sarah laughed within herself, saying, After I have waxen old shall I have pleasure, my lord
being old also?" Here was never a good word but one, viz.
that she called her husband lord, and this is recorded to her
eternal commendation, 1 *Pet* 3:6. Isaac then was not a child
of nature, but of the mere promise; so are all our graces. We

[144]

bring forth good things, as Sarah's dead womb brought forth a child.' (Trapp)

**V12: Therefore sprang there even of one, and him as good as dead, so many as the stars of the sky in multitude, and as the sand which is by the sea shore innumerable.**

Although the 'one' referred to here is Abraham, the previous verse shows that Sarah shared her husband's faith in the divine promise. 'If the Jews are now proud of their origin, they must look to its cause. Whatever they are is to be attributed to the faith of Abraham and Sarah. It follows from this that they cannot hold or defend the position which they have attained except on the basis of faith.' (Calvin) [*Gen* 15:5, 22:17; *Is* 51: 1, 2; *Rom* 4:16–21]

**V13: These all died in faith, not having received the promises, but having seen them afar off, and were persuaded of them, and embraced them, and confessed that they were strangers and pilgrims on the earth.**

**These all died in faith,** These verses which follow (*vv* 13–16) cannot apply to the antediluvians mentioned by the author, for they were not pilgrims in a strange land, and of course Enoch did not die! They rather point the lesson to be learned from the eminent example set by the founders of Israel. (*vv* 8–12) This verse conveys something more than an objective account of their obedience; it 'gives an internal picture of their mind and how they felt themselves to be, a consciousness which they preserved even up to death.' (A. B. Davidson)

**not having received the promises,** Since God was pleased on numerous occasions to confirm and expand the original promise made to Abraham, the plural is used here. Thus the

[145]

patriarchs believed the promises, which were centred in the Messiah through whom all the nations of the earth were to be blessed, yet they all died without having seen their fulfilment. If then they lived and died triumphantly on bare promises, how can those who have seen their fulfilment falter in their allegiance to Christ?

**but having seen them and greeted them from afar,** (RV) 'They were like pilgrims to the Holy City who see its towers and spires on the horizon, ecstatically point to the vision and shout their acclaim. This is all they had during their earthly lives.' (Lenski) [*John* 8:56]

**and having confessed that they were strangers and pilgrims on the earth.** (RV) 'The sum of the whole is, that they professed themselves called out of the world, separated from the world, as unto interest, design, rest, and reward; having placed their faith, hope, and trust, as unto all these things, in heaven above, and the good things to come.' (John Owen) [*Phil* 3:20]

*V*14: **For they that say such things declare plainly that they seek a country.**

In confessing themselves to be pilgrims on earth they declared that their true homeland was in heaven. 'Whosoever professes he has a Father in heaven, confesses himself a stranger on earth; hence there is in the heart an ardent longing, like that of a child among strangers, in want and grief, far from his fatherland.' (Luther, cited by A. R. Fausset)

*V*15: **And truly, if they had been mindful of that country from whence they came out, they might have had opportunity to have returned.**

[146]

Indeed if their thoughts had been fixed upon the country they had left then there was nothing to stop their return to it. Hence their exile was entirely voluntary. In the same way the readers had ample opportunity to end their pilgrimage of faith and return to the attractions of Judaism. But those who are truly called of God do not revert to the old life, not for lack of opportunity, but because they no longer desire it; whereas Demas returned to this present world for no other reason than that he still loved it! [2 *Tim* 4:10]

*V*16: **But now they desire a better country, that is, an heavenly: wherefore God is not ashamed to be called their God: for he hath prepared for them a city.**

**But now they desire a better country, that is, an heavenly:** 'In Hebrews as in Romans, we find nothing about a return to the land of Canaan. On the contrary, the writer stresses the *heavenly* character of the hope which the patriarchs cherished. It was not an earthly *land*, but a home (9:14, a "country of their own" [*patris*]) which is not earthly, but heavenly (*v* 16), a *city* "whose maker and builder is God" (*v* 10). The whole emphasis in this great faith chapter in Hebrews is that the faith of the Old Testament worthies was not earthly but heavenly.' (O. T. Allis, *Prophecy and the Church*, p. 101)

**wherefore God is not ashamed of them, to be called their God: for he hath prepared for them a city.** (RV) Since their life as pilgrims was an open declaration of their heavenly aspirations God is not ashamed to call himself their God. This proves that they ever live in fellowship with Him in the heavenly Jerusalem, for He is not the God of the dead but of the living. [cf. *Mark* 12:26, 27]

*V*17: **By faith Abraham, when he was tried, offered up Isaac: and he that had received the promises offered up his only begotten son,**

*V*18: **Of whom it was said, That in Isaac shall thy seed be called:**

As there could be no fulfilment of the divine promise without Isaac, the command to sacrifice his only son was the supreme test of Abraham's faith in God. [*Gen* 21:12; 22:1–18] 'God's usual manner of trying the faith of his people is, by causing the dispensations of his providence apparently to contradict his word, and requiring them still to rely upon that word, notwithstanding the apparent inconsistency. But in Abraham's trial, He proposed a test far more severe. For His own command, or word, was in direct contradiction to what he had before spoken; His injunction respecting the slaying of Isaac could, by no human method of reasoning, be reconciled to his promises respecting the future destinies of Abraham's family, of the Church, and of the world.' (Footnote by John King to Calvin's *Commentary on Genesis*, Book I, p. 562)

*V*19: **Accounting that God was able to raise him up, even from the dead; from whence also he received him in a figure.**

But Abraham refused to let his obedience to the command cancel his trust in the promise, for he reckoned that God was well able to raise up his son even from the dead. [*Gen* 22:5]

**from whence he did also in a parable receive him back.** (RV) Calvin's comment is a model of sober restraint. 'Although Isaac did not in fact rise from the dead, yet it seemed to be a kind of resurrection when he was snatched back suddenly and miraculously by the unexpected grace of God.'

*V*20: **By faith Isaac blessed Jacob and Esau concerning things to come.**

By faith Isaac believed the revelation which God made to him concerning the respective destinies of Jacob and Esau. And it was because he was fully conscious of the inspiration under which he had spoken that he made no attempt to revoke the blessing after the discovery of Jacob's deceit. [*Gen* 27:33] Instead he bowed to the divine decree even though it set aside the law of primogeniture and overruled his own inclinations. [*Rom* 9:10–13]

The readers also had received a revelation of things to come to which they must either give their unhesitating assent or else resign themselves to sharing Esau's bitter lot. [*Heb* 12:16, 17]

*V*21: **By faith Jacob, when he was a dying, blessed both the sons of Joseph; and worshipped, leaning upon the top of his staff.**

**By faith Jacob, when he was a dying, blessed each of the sons of Joseph;** (RV) It was faith which enabled Jacob when he lay dying in Egypt to predict the future inheritance of Ephraim and Manasseh in Canaan. [*Gen* 48:1 f.] The inference here is that those who do not lay hold of the promised blessings in faith cannot be the true descendants of the one who did.

**and worshipped, leaning upon the top of his staff.** This incident took place before the patriarchal benediction mentioned in the first part of the verse. [*Gen* 47:31] The difference between the LXX, 'upon the top of his staff,' and the Hebrew, 'upon the bed's head,' is only a matter of punctuation. The LXX read the unpointed Hebrew word M-TT-H as MATTEH, *staff*, whereas it is pointed in the Massoretic text as MITTAH, *bed*. In this instance it seems likely that the former is the more accurate reading, and it certainly makes better sense. As death drew near Jacob made Joseph swear that he would not leave his body in Egypt but that it would be taken to Canaan for burial there, and then he worshipped God, supporting

[149]

his now feeble frame upon his staff, which was '*the emblem of his pilgrim state.*' (A. R. Fausset) [*Gen* 32:10] Thus the fact that Jacob arranged to take possession of Canaan, 'as it were, by his dead body, was a very strong expression of his full persuasion that in due time his posterity should, according to the divine promise, possess it as an inheritance.' (John Brown)

*V*22: **By faith Joseph, when he died, made mention of the departing of the children of Israel; and gave commandment concerning his bones.**

At the end of his long life Joseph predicted the exodus of the children of Israel from Egypt, saying, 'God will surely visit you.' [*Gen* 50:24, 25] As one who was second only to Pharaoh himself his body might well have been laid to rest in some grand Egyptian tomb, but he entertained a far higher hope than this. For he publicly expressed his faith in the promised salvation by commanding that his bones should be taken with them and buried in Canaan. 'The plea of some of the Roman church from this place, for the preservation and veneration of relics, or the bones of saints departed, is weak unto the utmost contempt. For besides that this charge of Joseph concerning his bones and their disposal was singular, such a fruit of faith as could have no place in any other person, nor ever can there be the like occasion in the world, all that was done in compliance with that charge, was but the carrying of them shut up in a coffin into the land of Canaan, and there decently burying of them. To take an example from hence of digging men's bones out of their graves, of enshrining and placing them on altars, of carrying them up and down in procession, of adoring them with all signs of religious veneration, applying them unto miraculous operations, in curing diseases, casting out of devils, and the like, is fond and ridiculous.' (John Owen)

*V*23: **By faith Moses, when he was born, was hid three months of his parents, because they saw he was a proper child; and they were not afraid of the king's commandment.**

When Amram and Jochebed saw the beauty of Moses they resolved to defy the barbarous mandate which ordered the death of every son born of Hebrew parents, and they hid him in the house for three months, not fearing Pharaoh's impious decree. [*Exod* 2:2; *Acts* 4:19] Perhaps they believed the beauty of their child to be a special token of the divine favour which marked him out for a high destiny. (cf. *Acts* 7:20 RV margin, 'Moses . . . was fair unto God') However, it may well be that they received a more specific revelation of God's will concerning the child, but Scripture does not record it. In any case, as F. F. Bruce so justly observes, 'some appreciation of the divine purpose to be fulfilled through Moses is implied in his [the author's] ascription of faith to Amram and Jochebed.'

*V*24: **By faith Moses, when he was come to years, refused to be called the son of Pharaoh's daughter;**

*V*25: **Choosing rather to suffer affliction with the people of God, than to enjoy the pleasures of sin for a season;**

When Moses was 'full forty years old' he renounced the position he enjoyed in Egypt as the adopted son of Pharaoh's daughter in order to share the reproach of the people of God. [*Acts* 7:23] This was not the act of a pioneer revolutionary made in the interests of any earthly Utopia. It was not because he was of the same race that Moses chose to share the lot of a persecuted people but because he knew them to be 'the people of God.' Since his momentous decision was an act of faith in the promises of God it is very evident that recent political history can offer no parallel to it. 'The faith of Moses enabled

[151]

him to estimate aright the objects before him, and to forecast the future of the People of God, and oppose it to the temporary glory of sin. "Sin" in his case would have been apostasy, and there lies a delicate appeal to the Hebrews in his example.' (A. B. Davidson)

**the pleasures of sin** 'It is a common thing for a scripture to speak of a certain thing as if it were, and to say that it is, when it is only supposed to be so by others. For example, "There be gods many, and lords many" [I *Corinthians* 8:5]; not that there really were any such gods, but that by others they were reckoned so to be. Similarly in this text, he speaks according to the manner of men concerning the pleasures of sin, as they are reputed. . . . It is false pleasure, and what truer misery is there than false joy? It is like the pleasure of the man who receives much money, but it is all counterfeit, or the pleasure of the man who dreams of a feast and awakes so hungry and vexed that he could eat his dream. For this reason sin should be doubly hated, because it is ugly and false, because it defiles and mocks us.' (Ralph Venning, *The Plague of Plagues*, pp. 208–210)

*V*26: **Esteeming the reproach of Christ greater riches than the treasures in Egypt: for he had respect unto the recompence of the reward.**

**Accounting the reproach of Christ greater riches than the treasures of Egypt:** (RV) Geerhardus Vos points out that the phrase 'the reproach of Christ' is explained by the exhortation, 'Let us go forth therefore unto him without the camp, bearing his reproach.' [*Heb* 13:13] 'This reproach is thus seen to be a reproach which Christ Himself first bore and which we now bear together with Him. So we must similarly interpret the reproach of Christ borne by Moses. This does not imply that Moses had a prophetic knowledge of the sufferings of the future Messiah, but rather that the reproach which Moses bore was objectively identical with the reproach suffered by Christ and His people throughout the ages. This implies, therefore, that back of all the reproaches and sufferings which God's people have endured, stood Christ. How this appeared to Moses' own subjective consciousness is told us in 11:25, "choosing rather to share ill treatment with the people of God . . ."

**for he looked unto the recompense of reward.** (RV) The fleeting treasures of Egypt could not capture Moses' affections for he looked forward to an eternal inheritance. [*Heb* 11:6] 'Let the things of this world be increased and multiplied into the greatest measures and degrees imaginable, it alters not their kind. – They are temporary, fading, and perishing still; such as will stand men in no stead on their greatest occasions, nor with respect unto eternity.' (John Owen)

*V*27: **By faith he forsook Egypt, not fearing the wrath of the king: for he endured, as seeing him who is invisible.**

The strange attempt to reconcile this verse with Moses' fearful flight to Midian should be abandoned. [*Exod* 2:14, 15] It must refer to the events associated with the Exodus which is here ascribed to the faith of Moses because it was accomplished under his inspired leadership. 'Not fearing the wrath of the king' describes his fearless demeanour before Pharaoh as he repeatedly demanded the release of God's people. [cf. *Exod* 10: 28, 29] It was by 'seeing him who is invisible' that Moses thus withstood the wrath of this earthly potentate, and was able to lead the children of Israel out of Egypt without fear of what might be done to prevent their escape.

*V*28: **Through faith he kept the passover, and the sprinkling of blood, lest he that destroyed the firstborn should touch them.**

Moses 'instituted the passover' (RV margin) for no other reason
than that God had commanded it. He instructed the people to
offer the appointed sacrifice and to sprinkle their door posts
with the blood, for he was fully persuaded that this unusual
measure would protect them from the destroyer as he passed
through the land in terrible judgment. [*Exod* 12] 'That which
God would for ever instruct the church in by this ordinance is,
that unless we are sprinkled with the blood of Christ, our
paschal Lamb, no other privilege can secure us from eternal
destruction. – Though a man had been really an Israelite, and
had with others made himself ready that night for a departure,
which was a high profession of faith, yet if the lintel and posts
of his door had not been sprinkled with blood, he would have
been destroyed. And on the other hand, where there is this
sprinkling of blood, be the danger never so great or so near,
there shall be certain deliverance. "The blood of sprinkling
speaks better things than the blood of Abel."' (John Owen)
[*John* 1:29; 1 *Cor* 5:7]

*V*29: **By faith they passed through the Red sea as by dry
land: which the Egyptians assaying to do were drowned.**

As John Owen notes, 'the whole is denominated from the
better part,' for the vast majority of those who passed safely
through the Red Sea later perished miserably in the wilderness
because of their unbelief. [*Exod* 14:11; 1 *Cor* 10:5; *Heb* 3:7–19]
But on this occasion the temporal deliverance of the many was
effected by the saving faith of the few: e.g. Moses, Aaron,
Caleb, and Joshua. [*Rom* 9:6]

**which the Egyptians assaying to do were swallowed up.**
(RV) '*Rash presumption* mistaken by many for *faith*: with
similar presumption many rush into eternity. The same thing
done by the believer and by the unbeliever is not the same
thing. What was *faith* in Israel was *presumption* in the Egyptians.' (A. R. Fausset)

[154]

*V*30: **By faith the walls of Jericho fell down, after they were compassed about seven days.**

The next example of faith which is celebrated by the author is separated from the exodus by an interval of forty years. This period is passed over in silence because he regards the wanderings in the wilderness as the years of unbelief. A signal instance of the power of united faith is provided by the fall of Jericho, for after Joshua and the children of Israel had marched silently round this apparently impregnable citadel for seven days its mighty walls at last collapsed before their triumphant shout of faith. The Hebrews are called to a similar exercise of faith in the power of God to conquer all the bastions of unbelief. [*Josh* 6; *Zech* 4:6, 7; 2 *Cor* 10:3-5]

*V*31: **By faith the harlot Rahab perished not with them that believed not, when she had received the spies with peace.**

No doubt the surprising inclusion of Rahab in the roll of those whose faith is specially praised is an implied rebuke to the readers. [*Josh* 2] For if an Amorite harlot believed the reports she had heard of the God of Israel so that 'she perished not with them that were disobedient' (RV), then how can the children of the covenant renounce their interest in the promised Messiah? Calvin says that she is only described as 'the harlot' in order to magnify the grace of God in reclaiming her from such a disgraceful past, for it is certain that 'her faith is the evidence of her repentance.' [*Josh* 6:25; *Jas* 2:25] Indeed she later married a prince of Judah, and shares with 'Ruth the Moabitess' an honoured place in the genealogy of the Saviour Himself. [*Matt* 1:5]

**when she had received the spies** 'Whom to secure she told a lie, which was ill done. The apostle commends her faith in God, but not her deceit toward her neighbour.' (Trapp)

*V*32: **And what shall I more say? for the time would fail me to tell of Gedeon, and of Barak, and of Samson, and of Jephthae; of David also, and Samuel, and of the prophets:**

Although the list is far from exhausted, lack of time forces the author rapidly to sum up the achievements (*vv* 32–34) and the sufferings of faith (*vv* 35–38) in a brilliant final paragraph. However, the order remains roughly chronological, for apart from David, all those named here belong to the period of the Judges, while some of the later descriptions appear to allude to the courageous endurance of the Maccabean martyrs. By this subtle device the readers are faced with a long line of witnesses who remained faithful to their calling. Will they now waver in theirs?

*V*33: **Who through faith subdued kingdoms, wrought righteousness, obtained promises, stopped the mouths of lions,**

*V*34: **Quenched the violence of fire, escaped the edge of the sword, out of weakness were made strong, waxed valiant in fight, turned to flight the armies of the aliens.**

A powerful impression is produced by the cumulative effect of this swift inventory of faith's exploits. With all the skill of an orator, the writer invites them to 'See what faith has wrought!' Some of the items are readily identified; others have a more general reference.

**Who through faith subdued kingdoms,** As Joshua conquered Canaan, and David brought Edom, Moab, Ammon, and Syria under tribute.

**wrought righteousness,** This probably refers to the righteous rule exercised by those mentioned in the previous verse.

[156]

**obtained promises,** The Old Testament saints did live to see many promises fulfilled, though they died without having received the fulfilment of the Messianic promises. (cf. *vv* 13, 39)

**stopped the mouths of lions,** An obvious reference to Daniel. [*Dan* 6:22]

**Quenched the violence of fire,** Here Shadrach, Meshach, and Abed-nego at once spring to mind. [*Dan* 3:27]

**escaped the edge of the sword,** Either in battle or as David did from Saul and Elijah from Jezebel.

**out of weakness were made strong,** Samson seems to be in view here. [*Judg* 16:28]

**waxed valiant in fight,** Israel's notable victories were the fruit of faith in the divine promises.

**turned to flight the armies of the aliens.** No doubt this includes the triumphs of the Maccabees, though it is impossible to overlook an allusion to Gideon's rout of the Midianites. [*Judg* 7:20, 21]

*V*35: **Women received their dead raised to life again: and others were tortured, not accepting deliverance; that they might obtain a better resurrection:**

The writer now begins a harrowing account of the sufferings of the faithful. 'There was never any greater instance of the degeneracy of human nature unto the image and likeness of the devil than this, that so many of them have been found, and that in high places of power, emperors, kings, judges, and priests, who were not satisfied to take away the lives of the true worshippers of God by the sword, or by such other ways as they slew the worst of malefactors, but invented all kinds of hellish tortures whereby to destroy them.' (John Owen) In this verse an extreme contrast is drawn between the women who were delivered from the suffering of bereavement 'by a resurrection' (RV) of their dead, and the refusal of the Maccabean martyrs to recant under the most fiendish tortures because they looked for a 'better resurrection' than a mere respite from earthly suffering. [1 *Kings* 17:17–24; 2 *Kings* 4:18–37; 2 *Macc* 7:9, 11, 14; 2 *Cor* 4:17, 18]

*V*36: **And others had trial of cruel mockings and scourgings, yea, moreover of bonds and imprisonment:**

*V*37: **They were stoned, they were sawn asunder, were tempted, were slain with the sword: they wandered about in sheepskins and goatskins; being destitute, afflicted, tormented;**

Others whose sufferings fell short of martyrdom, nevertheless endured cruel mockery, scourging, bonds, and imprisonment [e.g. 1 *Kings* 22:24–27; *Jer* 20:2, 37:15], while some were stoned, sawn asunder, or slain with the sword. In view of the context many regard the words 'were tempted' as an incongruous insertion, but A. B. Davidson points out that the MS. authority favours this reading and that 'the reference must be to cruel tortures practised on men to procure apostasy.' According to tradition Jeremiah was stoned to death in Egypt, and Isaiah was 'sawn asunder' during Manasseh's evil reign. [For scriptural examples, see 2 *Chron* 24:20–22; *Jer* 26: 23] The same fidelity to God forced others to wander about like wild animals, destitute of even the common necessities of life.

*V*38: **(Of whom the world was not worthy:) they wandered in deserts, and in mountains, and in dens and caves of the earth.**

(Of whom the world was not worthy:) 'They were fitter to be set as stars in heaven, and be before the Lord in his glory. The world was not worthy of their presence, and yet they were not thought worthy to live in the world.' (Trapp)

'caves (OPAIS) – "chinks." Palestine, from its hilly character, abounds in *fissures* and caves, affording shelter to the persecuted, as the fifty hid by Obadiah and Elijah [1 *Kings* 18:4, 13; 19:8, 13]; Mattathias and his sons [1 *Macc* 2:28, 29]; Judas Maccabeus [2 *Macc* 5:27].' (A. R. Fausset)

*V*39: **And these all, having obtained a good report through faith, received not the promise:**

*V*40: **God having provided some better thing for us, that they without us should not be made perfect.**

Even though all these heroes obtained a good report through faith, they did not receive the fulfilment of the promise during their life on earth. For 'God had something better in view for us, (and so purposed) that they should not attain the Perfection apart from us.' (W. Manson's translation) Thus they could not reach 'perfection' without us because the fulfilment of that promise awaited our day! [cf. *Heb* 12:23] 'If those on whom the great life of grace had not yet shone showed such patience in bearing their ills, what effect ought the full light of the Gospel to have on us? A tiny spark of light led them to heaven, but now that the sun of righteousness shines on us what excuse shall we offer if we still hold to the earth?' (Calvin)

# CHAPTER TWELVE

***V*1: Wherefore seeing we also are compassed about with so great a cloud of witnesses, let us lay aside every weight, and the sin which doth so easily beset us, and let us run with patience the race that is set before us.**

**Therefore let us also,** (RV) 'Therefore' shows that this admonition is based on the examples afforded by those who through faith 'obtained a good report.' [*Heb* 11:4–40]

**seeing we are compassed about with so great a cloud of witnesses,** (RV) This does not mean that this host of witnesses are the heavenly spectators of what takes place in the earthly arena. 'The souls of the saints are at rest, they are no longer concerned about the trials that occur on earth. The Scriptures teach that they behold the heavenly glories and say nothing about their beholding and watching earthly events. These saints are not "witnesses" that see our faith and testify about us; God does not ask them to testify about us. They are witnesses whose life, works, sufferings, death attest their own faith, testify to us through the pages of Holy Writ and in other history that they were true men of faith indeed (the faith defined in 11:1).' (Lenski)

**lay aside every weight,** (RV) As the athlete disciplines himself to discard everything that would impede his progress in the contest for which he has entered, so also every weight must be

[160]

laid aside in the Christian race. An immoderate use of that which is not in itself sinful can become a great hindrance to the Christian. 'So many professing Christians never seem to have any "weights," and we never see them *drop* anything. Ah, the fact is, they have never entered the race. O to be able to say with Paul, "I count all things but loss for the excellency of the knowledge of Christ Jesus my Lord." [*Phil* 3:8].' (Arthur Pink)

**and the sin which doth closely cling to us,** (RV margin) 'This sin is compared to a loose garment which readily comes round the limbs of the racer, and, entangling him, diminishes his speed, retards him in his course. . . . What that sin was, it is not difficult to discover. It is the sin, to guard them against which is the great object of the whole of the Epistle – the yielding to the "evil heart of unbelief, in departing from the living God." . . . There is no prayer the Christian needs to put up more frequently than, "Lord, increase my faith; help my unbelief." Whatever darkens our views or shakes our confidence with respect to any of the great principles of our Christian faith, cuts the very sinews of dutiful exertion, so that it becomes very difficult, or rather altogether impossible, to persevere in running "the race that is set before us."' (John Brown)

**and let us run with patience the race that is set before us,** (RV) 'Patience' is not passivity, but rather 'patient endurance.' (Davidson) It is the lack of stamina which distinguishes the would-be competitor from the successful athlete. In the Christian race there are no prizes for those who do not persevere to the end of their course. [Contrast *Acts* 20:24; 2 *Tim* 4:7, 8]

*V*2: **Looking unto Jesus the author and finisher of our faith; who for the joy that was set before him endured the cross, despising the shame, and is set down at the right hand of the throne of God.**

**Looking unto Jesus** The author now reveals the secret of Christian perseverance. The strength to run the race is only found by fixing the gaze upon the great object of faith. 'Nor shall we endure any longer than whilst the eye of our faith is fixed on him. From him alone do we derive our refreshments in all our trials.' (John Owen)

**the author and finisher of our faith;** Here 'Christ is called the "Author and Perfecter of faith," He is represented as the One who takes precedence in faith and is thus the perfect Exemplar of it. The pronoun "our" does not correspond to anything in the original, and may well be omitted. Christ in the days of His flesh trod undeviatingly the path of faith, and as the Perfecter has brought it to a perfect end in His own Person. Thus He is the leader of all others who tread that path.' (W. E. Vine)

**who for the joy that was set before him endured the cross, despising the shame,** 'Our Lord believed the promises made to Him: He believed that He was to "be exalted, and extolled, and made very high" – that He was to "see of the travail of His soul, and be satisfied" – that "His soul should not be left in the separate state, nor His body see corruption" – that "God would show Him the path of life;" and, believing this, He "did not fail, nor was He discouraged;" – He persevered, amid inconceivable difficulties and sufferings, till He could say, "It is finished."' (John Brown)

**and is set down at the right hand of the throne of God.** In this verse the splendid isolation of our Lord's human name underlines His willing endurance of those sufferings by which He won the salvation of His people, yet faith recognizes 'that same Jesus' as the One whom God hath made 'both Lord and Christ.' [*Acts* 2:36] He who once suffered on earth now rules from heaven. [*Matt* 28:18] The Hebrews must believe this however much present circumstances may appear to contradict it. [*Heb* 12:3 f.] And so must we!

***V3*: For consider him that endured such contradiction of sinners against himself, lest ye be wearied and faint in your minds.**

**For consider him that hath endured such gainsaying of sinners against himself,** (ARV) Let them reflect upon what it meant for the *sinless* One patiently to bear the implacable hatred of *sinners* against Himself. [*Is* 53:7]

**that ye wax not weary, fainting in your souls.** (ARV) 'The constant consideration of Christ in his sufferings is the best means to keep up faith unto its due exercise in all times of trial.' (John Owen) [1 *Pet* 2:21-24]

***V4*: Ye have not yet resisted unto blood, striving against sin.**

Unlike 'the captain of their salvation' the Hebrews have not as yet suffered death in striving against sin, though they have 'endured a great fight of afflictions' because of their confession of faith in Him. [*Heb* 10:32-34] The particular sin of unbelief to which these unexpected hardships had exposed them is here personified as a formidable foe who must be resisted even at the cost of life itself. 'This sin would win if in fear of blood the readers would relinquish their faith; it would be vanquished if the readers, unafraid of a bloody death, held fast to their faith.' (Lenski)

***V5*: And ye have forgotten the exhortation which speaketh unto you as unto children, My son, despise not thou the chastening of the Lord, nor faint when thou art rebuked of him:**

*V*6: **For whom the Lord loveth he chasteneth, and scourgeth every son whom he receiveth.**

The readers were repining under the opposition they encountered because they had forgotten the scripture that addresses them as children who must receive with meekness the chastening of their heavenly Father. [*Prov* 3:11, 12. Also *Job* 5:17; *Ps* 94:12; *Rev* 3:19] Although the hard-hearted steels himself against feeling the stroke, and the faint-hearted reels under it, the child of God is neither to despise correction nor to despair when he is reproved, or else he will fail to profit from the experience.

**For whom the Lord loveth he chasteneth, and scourgeth every son whom he receiveth.** God punishes His enemies; He chastens His children. The one is the judicial infliction of His wrath; the other is the proof of His parental love. 'The same hand – but not the same character – gives the stroke, to the godly and the ungodly. The scourge of the Judge is widely different from the rod of the Father.' (Charles Bridges, *Commentary on Proverbs*, p. 31 n.) Moreover, this fatherly discipline pertains only to the present life. 'There is no chastisement in heaven, nor in hell. Not in heaven, because there is no sin; not in hell, because there is no amendment. Chastisement is a companion of them that *are in the way*, and of them only.' (John Owen)

*V*7: **If ye endure chastening, God dealeth with you as with sons; for what son is he whom the father chasteneth not?**

'Corrections are pledges of our adoption and badges of our sonship. One Son God hath without sin, but none without sorrow. As God corrects none but his own, so all that are his shall be sure to have it; and they shall take it for a favour too, I *Cor* 11:32.' (Trapp)

*V*8: **But if ye be without chastisement, whereof all are partakers, then are ye bastards, and not sons.**

'Saints, saith God, think not that I hate you, because I thus chide you. He that escapes reprehension may suspect his adoption. God had one Son without corruption, but no son without correction. A gracious soul may look through the darkest cloud, and see a God smiling on him.' (Thomas Brooks, *Precious Remedies against Satan's Devices*, pp. 85–86)

*V*9: **Furthermore we have had fathers of our flesh which corrected us, and we gave them reverence: shall we not much rather be in subjection unto the Father of spirits, and live?**

'This comparison is made in several parts. The first is that if we give so much reverence to the fathers of whom we are born after the flesh that we submit to their discipline, much more honour is due to God who is our spiritual Father. The second is that the discipline by which fathers bring up their children is only useful for this present life, but God looks further to sanctify us for eternal life. Thirdly, mortal men chastise their children as they think good, but God applies His discipline with the wisest purpose and the highest wisdom so that there is nothing in it that is out of control.' (Calvin)

**and live?** 'We are reminded by this that nothing is more fatal to us than to refuse to give ourselves in obedience to God.' (Calvin)

*V*10: **For they verily for a few days chastened us after their own pleasure; but he for our profit, that we might be partakers of his holiness.**

'The fathers of our flesh' chastened us according to what 'seemed good to them' (RV), but God with unerring wisdom designs it for our spiritual good. 'What the Author means to bring out by saying that the chastisement of earthly parents is for a few days, is the brevity and comparative unimportance of our connection with our natural parents; their chastisement is for a short time as the duration of our relation to them is short, and indeed their chastisement, if wise, has in view to make us able to be independent of them; God's chastening has another view, to make us partakers of His holiness, to unite us to Him in character and likeness more and more. It is not the duration of the chastisement that is the point of the passage; it is the duration of our relation in each case to Him who chastens.' (A. B. Davidson)

*V*11 : **Now no chastening for the present seemeth to be joyous, but grievous: nevertheless afterward it yieldeth the peaceable fruit of righteousness unto them which are exercised thereby.**

To be sure, no chastening is regarded as an enjoyable experience at the time, but rather grievous. Later, however, it yields the peaceful fruit of righteousness to those who have been exercised by it. The stoical endurance of that which was intended to be *felt* can never produce such fruit! [*Is* 9 : 8–12] 'We can never find any benefit in chastisements, unless we are "exercised" by them; that is, that all our graces are stirred up by them unto a holy, constant exercise. – For hereby alone do they yield "the peaceable fruit of righteousness."' (John Owen)

*V*12 : **Wherefore lift up the hands which hang down, and the feeble knees;**

*V*13 : **And make straight paths for your feet, lest that which is lame be turned out of the way; but let it rather be healed.**

The practical application of this teaching is couched in language which is evidently taken from *Isaiah* 35:3 and *Proverbs* 4:26. In verse 12 the bracing of the body stands for the spiritual resolution with which they are to meet adversity. Instead of wilting under chastisement, they are to 'straighten out the limp hands and the paralysed knees.' (Lenski)

**And make straight paths for your feet, that that which is lame be not put out of joint, but rather be healed.** (RV margin) No advance in the Christian way is possible while the community halts between two opinions, for they cannot follow the straight path of grace until they make a final break with Judaism. [1 *Kings* 18:21] 'Inconsistency and vacillation in the general body of the church would create a way so difficult for the lame, that their lameness would become dislocation, and they would perish from the way; on the other hand, the habit of going in a plain path would restore them to soundness.' (A. B. Davidson)

*V*14: **Follow peace with all men, and holiness, without which no man shall see the Lord.**

The following verses (*vv* 14–17) set forth the indispensable conditions for receiving the promised blessings of the gospel. Although peace with all men will persistently elude their grasp, yet they must strive after it, so long as it is never enjoyed at the expense of that 'sanctification' (RV) without which no man shall see the Lord. [*Rom* 12:18] 'Peace with men is not to be followed nor practised at any such rate. We must eternally bid defiance unto that peace with men which is inconsistent with peace with God.' (John Owen)

**and holiness,** All 'man's happiness here is his holiness, and his holiness shall hereafter be his happiness. Christ hath there-

[167]

fore broke the devil's yoke from off our necks, that his Father
might have better service from our hearts.' (Thomas Brooks)
As they had been separated unto God by a profession of faith
in Christ, so they are to live the life 'befitting those so separated.' (W. E. Vine) [Matt 5:8] 'We may follow peace with
men, and not attain it; but if we follow holiness, we shall as
assuredly see the Lord, as we shall come short of this without
it.' (John Owen)

V15: **Looking diligently lest any man fail of the grace of
God; lest any root of bitterness springing up trouble
you, and thereby many be defiled;**

**Looking carefully whether there be any man that falleth
back from the grace of God,** (RV margin) It would be foolish to infer from this that the saints of God can fall from
grace and be lost, because the author has in view only the
'*phenomenal* aspect of religion.' (G. Vos) He is making the
simple point that anyone who abandons his profession of
faith in Christ in favour of a return to Judaism is left behind
in the wilderness of unbelief, and it is to guard against this
danger that he exhorts them all to be overseers of one another.
[Heb 3:12 f.]

**lest any root of bitterness springing up trouble you, and
thereby the many be defiled;** (RV) Such a man would be
like the springing up of a bitter root which spreads its defilement to the whole congregation, thus making it unfit to
worship God. [Deut 29:18; Josh 7:25] 'So long as it is under
the earth it cannot be remedied, but when it "springs up," it
must be dealt with boldly. Still remember the caution [Matt
13:26-30] as to rooting out *persons*. No such danger can arise
in rooting out bad *principles*.' (A. R. Fausset) [1 Cor 15:33]

V16: **Lest there be any fornicator, or profane person, as
Esau, who for one morsel of meat sold his birthright.**

*V*17: **For ye know how that afterward, when he would have inherited the blessing, he was rejected: for he found no place of repentance, though he sought it carefully with tears.**

**Lest there be any fornicator, or profane person, as Esau,** The spiritual safety of the congregation depends upon the vigilance of its members, as the presence of one 'troubler' endangers the purity of 'the many.' The reference is not to sexual immorality, which is dealt with later in the Epistle [13:4 RV], but to the peril of religious infidelity. The 'fornication' that the author has in mind is illustrated by the profane choice of Esau, who forfeited the blessing of God in favour of a paltry secular benefit. Thus the word 'fornicator' is 'used here in the Biblical sense of idolator.' (R. V. G. Tasker)

**who for one mess of meat sold his own birthright.** (RV) As the first-born, Esau possessed spiritual privileges which were distinctively his own, until he rashly bartered them away for a miserable morsel of meat – such a 'cheap meal,' says Calvin, as that 'by which Satan habitually lures the reprobate.' [*Gen* 25:29–34]

**For ye know how that afterward,** Even though he later desired to inherit the blessing it was all to no avail. 'As in the believer's case, so in the unbeliever's, there is an "afterward" coming, when the believer shall look on his past griefs, and the unbeliever on his past joys, in a very different light from that in which they were respectively viewed at the time. Cf. "nevertheless *afterward*," etc., *v* 11, with it here.' (A. R. Fausset) [*Gen* 27:34, 38]

**when he would have inherited the blessing, he was rejected: for he found no place of repentance,** Because the damage was done Esau gained nothing from his belated change of mind. 'Esau came too short because too late. Think of the uncertainty of the gales of grace, and be nimble.' (Trapp) [*Prov* 1:24–32; *Is* 55:6; 2 *Cor* 6:2]

**though he sought it carefully with tears.** 'Sin may be the occasion of great sorrow, where there is no sorrow for sin; as it was with Esau. – Men may rue that in the consequents, which yet they like well enough in the causes.' (John Owen) [2 *Cor* 7:9, 10]

*V*18: **For ye are not come unto the mount that might be touched, and that burned with fire, nor unto blackness, and darkness, and tempest,**

*V*19: **And the sound of a trumpet, and the voice of words; which voice they that heard intreated that the word should not be spoken to them any more:**

The issue facing the readers is now crystallized in one magnificent sentence. (*vv* 18–24) As the superiority of the new covenant infinitely transcends that of the old economy which it has superseded, so those who despise the grace so fully exhibited in it will be visited by sanctions even more severe than those which attended the giving of the law. [*Heb* 2:2–4] The welcome absence of the awesome sensible phenomena which characterized the Sinaitic revelation must not lead them to doubt the ultimate reality of that supersensible world to which they have been brought by the gospel. For the very same voice which spoke to the people 'from the mount that might be touched' now addresses them from heaven itself! Well might the author earnestly urge them to 'See that ye refuse not him that speaketh.' (*v* 25) 'The material mountain is an emblem of its earthly and sensible character: the clouds and darkness, of its obscurity; and the tempest and flaming fire, the fearful trumpet, and yet more awful voice, of the strictness of its precepts, and of the severity of its sanctions; – the holiness and the justice of Jehovah being plainly revealed, while but a very dim and imperfect manifestation was made of His grace and mercy.' (John Brown)

**which voice they that heard intreated that the word should not be spoken to them any more:** As the people heard the direct speech of God from out of the fire and darkness which surrounded the mount they were stricken with terror, for 'the speaking of the law doth immediately discover the invincible necessity of a mediator between God and sinners.' (John Owen) [*Exod* 20:19; *Deut* 5:25]

*V*20: (**For they could not endure that which was commanded, And if so much as a beast touch the mountain, it shall be stoned, or thrust through with a dart:**

*V*21: **And so terrible was the sight, that Moses said, I exceedingly fear and quake:)**

'The effect of this terror extended itself unto the meanest of beasts, and unto the best of men,' and, argues John Owen, if the 'mediator himself of the old covenant was not able to sustain the dread and terror of the law: how desperate then are their hopes who would yet be saved by Moses!' [*Exod* 19: 10–13]

**it shall be stoned;** (RV) The best texts omit 'or thrust through with a dart.' They were instructed 'to kill the trespassing beast from a distance in that to touch it would involve transgressing the barrier.' (F. F. Bruce's footnote giving the substance of a comment by A. H. McNeile)

Although the words attributed to Moses in verse 21 are not an exact quotation from the Old Testament, there is no need to doubt that they accurately represent his state of mind on that occasion. He gives expression to similar sentiments in *Deut* 9: 19, on which Conybeare and Howson sensibly remark, 'It was the *remembrance* of this terrible sight which caused Moses to say this; much more must he have been terrified by the reality.' (Goold's footnote in Owen)

*V*22: **But ye are come unto mount Sion, and unto the city of the living God, the heavenly Jerusalem, and to an innumerable company of angels,**

*V*23: **To the general assembly and church of the first-born, which are written in heaven, and to God the Judge of all, and to the spirits of just men made perfect,**

*V*24: **And to Jesus the mediator of the new covenant, and to the blood of sprinkling, that speaketh better things than that of Abel.**

**But ye are come unto Mount Sion, and unto the city of the living God, the heavenly Jerusalem,** Mount Zion is here spiritualized to suggest an image of that heavenly realm to which the Hebrews have been brought by grace. Thus in leaving Mount Sinai for Mount Zion they have exchanged the sensuous for the spiritual; the place of temporal manifestation for the eternal abode of the righteous; and the dread sense of separation from God for the gracious privilege of unbroken communion with God through Jesus Christ. 'As Jerusalem was distinguished into two cities, the superior and the inferior; so is the Church into triumphant and militant; yet both make up but one city of the living God.' (Trapp) [*Heb* 11:10, 16]

**and to myriads of angels in festal assembly;** (Lenski) 'Sinai, too, had its angels, but they did not appear in festal assembly, see *Acts* 7:53 and *Gal* 3:19. The word "myriads" or ten thousands is repeatedly used with reference to angels

[*Dan* 7:10; *Jude* 14; *Rev* 5:11]. Since Christ has entered heaven after his work of redemption, the whole angel world rings with festal panegyrics [*Rev* 5:1-12].' (Lenski)

**and to a church of first-born enrolled in (the) heavens;** (Lenski) Those who still tread the pilgrim path on earth may rejoice in the knowledge that their names are already written in heaven, and that before long they will join that vast company which forms the church triumphant. [*Luke* 10:20; *Rev* 21:27] 'All the people of Christ are the "firstborn" children of God, through their union with Him who is The First-born *par excellence*; their birthright is not to be bartered away, as was Esau's.' (F. F. Bruce)

**and to a Judge, God of all;** (Lenski) The God of all creation is the Judge who will vindicate the cause of the righteous and speedily avenge the wrongs inflicted upon them by their persecutors. [*Luke* 18:7, 8] 'In Jesus Christ believers are delivered from all discouraging dread and terror, in the consideration of God as a judge; such, I mean, as befell the people at Sinai in the giving of the law. They now behold all his glory in the face of Jesus Christ; which makes it amiable and desirable unto them.' (John Owen) [2 *Cor* 4:6; 2 *Tim* 4:8]

**and to the spirits of just men made perfect,** 'The souls of the just when separated from their bodies, do not wander up and down in this world, nor hover about the sepulchres where their bodies lie; nor are they detained in any purgatory, in order to their more perfect purification; nor do they fall asleep in a benumbed stupid state: but do forthwith pass into glory, and are immediately with the Lord.' (John Flavel, *Works*, Vol. III, p. 38) [*Luke* 23:43]

**And to Jesus the mediator of the new covenant,** The 'Mediator of the Sion covenant is better than the mediator at Sinai, and more able to promote the holiness required by it. Believers have not now access unto, or dependence on, a

Moses, a mere man, and a servant, declaring God's will, only a sinner himself, trembling in his office, and weary of his clients, and whose ministry is vanishing, as his person dying; but unto God the Son himself incarnate, a Son-mediator, making sons, and bringing them nearer to God, satisfying the law for them, and writing it on their hearts; above all sin himself, though a sacrifice for it, who is able to save to the uttermost, for that he ever liveth to intercede for them, *ch* 1: 1–3; 3:6; 7:26; *Rev* 1:13. He is the Mediator, not of a literal, dark, terrible, charging and condemning, temporary and vanishing, covenant; but of the most spiritual, lightsome, gracious, justifying, sanctifying, and everlasting testamental dispensation of God, more effectually influencing souls to holiness than the old, *ch* 8:10, 11; 2 *Cor* 3:6; 5:19.' (Poole)

**and to the blood of sprinkling, that speaketh better things than that of Abel.** Abel and Jesus were both slain by wicked hands, but whereas Abel's blood cried for vengeance on him by whom it was shed, that of Jesus pleads for the pardon of such guilty sinners, and so 'speaketh better things than that of Abel.' [*Gen* 4:10; *Luke* 23:34] It is here called 'the blood of sprinkling' since it cleanses only those to whom it is applied in faith. [1 *John* 1:7]

**V25: See that ye refuse not him that speaketh. For if they escaped not who refused him that spake on earth, much more shall not we escape, if we turn away from him that speaketh from heaven:**

The preceding comparison is enforced by a solemn warning not to capitulate to the prompting of unbelief which could stifle that voice which still speaks to them in grace from heaven. For – 'If those who disobeyed Jehovah, speaking on earth respecting an earthly and temporary economy, were punished, surely much more will they be punished who disobey Him speaking from heaven, respecting a spiritual and everlasting order of things.' (John Brown) [*Heb* 2:2 f; 10:29]

*V*26: **Whose voice then shook the earth: but now he hath promised, saying, Yet once more I shake not the earth only, but also heaven.**

*V*27: **And this word, Yet once more, signifieth the removing of those things that are shaken, as of things that are made, that those things which cannot be shaken may remain.**

Although the majority of commentators regard this passage as referring to the events which will accompany the second advent, John Owen rightly insists that it is more fitly applied to the momentous changes which were brought about by His first coming. 'Take the words metaphorically for great changes, commotions, and alterations in the world, and so also were they accomplished in him and his coming. No such alteration had been made in the world since the creation of it, as was then, and in what ensued thereon . . . It is therefore the *heavens of Mosaical worship*, and the Judaical church-state, with the *earth of their political state* belonging thereunto, that are here intended. These were they that were shaken at the coming of Christ, and so shaken, as shortly after to be removed and taken away, for the introduction of the more heavenly worship of the gospel, and the immovable evangelical church-state. This was the greatest commotion and alteration that God ever made in the heavens and earth of the church, and which was to be made once only. This was far more great and glorious than the shaking of the earth at the giving of the law.' Moreover, it is only this interpretation which does justice to the alternatives which faced the first readers of the Epistle. 'It is by the gospel from heaven that God shook to pieces the civil and ecclesiastical state of the Jewish nation, and introduced a new state of the church that cannot be removed, shall never be changed for any other on earth, but shall remain till it be made perfect in heaven.' (Matthew Henry, cited by Pink)

*V*28: **Wherefore we receiving a kingdom which cannot be moved, let us have grace, whereby we may serve God acceptably with reverence and godly fear:**

*V*29: **For our God is a consuming fire.**

'Let us have grace' is more accurately rendered 'let us be thankful.' (Arndt-Gingrich) The grace which has invested them with all the privileges of citizenship in an unshakeable kingdom must constrain an overwhelming sense of gratitude to God. This will find its natural expression in service that is well-pleasing to Him because it proceeds from those whose lives are permeated by 'godly fear and awe.' (RV margin) This reverential fear of God accompanies every genuine experience of His redeeming love, for the nearer we are brought to God by grace, the greater will be our sense of the infinite gulf which separates the creature from the Creator. [cf. *Is* 6:1 f.]

**For our God is a consuming fire.** These words are taken from *Deut* 4:24 which warns Israel that their covenant relationship with God ('*our* God') would not protect them from the devouring fire of divine judgment if they incurred His jealousy by lapsing into the sin of idolatry. An abiding consciousness of the ineffable holiness of God offers the best deterrent against the commission of sin, and therefore every child of grace prays, 'Unite my heart to fear thy name,' for he knows that it is impossible to combine a love of sin with a love for God. [*Ps* 86:11] 'Even those who stand highest in the love and favour of God, and have the fullest assurance thereof and of their interest in Him as *their* God, ought, notwithstanding, to fear Him as a sin-avenging God and a consuming fire.' (Ezekiel Hopkins, quoted by Pink)

# CHAPTER THIRTEEN

*V*1: **Let brotherly love continue.**

Whenever this command is 'more honoured in the breach than the observance,' Christianity ceases to exist, for God refuses to accept the professed service of those who are without love for the brethren. Hence the need to insist upon the *continuance* of this love! The primary importance of this injunction makes it unnecessary to imagine that it was called forth by any particular situation. It is everywhere insisted upon throughout the New Testament. [e.g. *John* 13:34; *Rom* 13:8; 1 *Cor* 13:1–13; 1 *Thess* 4:9; 1 *Pet* 1:22; 1 *John* 2:10; 3:11, 23; 4:7, 11, 12, 21] In deploring the decline of such love in his day, John Owen says that 'it is marvellous how any men can persuade themselves that they are Christians, and yet be not only strangers, but enemies unto this love.'

*V*2: **Be not forgetful to entertain strangers: for thereby some have entertained angels unawares.**

A readiness to welcome travellers and a compassionate concern for those under affliction are two ways in which this brotherly love is to be manifested. (*vv* 2, 3) They must not neglect to offer hospitality to strangers for in so doing 'some have entertained angels unawares,' not as though they will receive such supernatural visitors as Abraham once did, but they may well find that some of their guests resemble angels in proving to be true messengers of God to them. [*Gen* 18] '*Not unconscious* of the duty, they have *unconsciously* brought on themselves the blessing.' (A. R. Fausset)

*V*3: **Remember them that are in bonds, as bound with them; and them which suffer adversity, as being yourselves also in the body.**

Those who are imprisoned or who suffer adversity of any kind for the sake of Christ and His gospel must continue to command the sympathy and succour of their fellow Christians. [*Heb* 10:32–34]

**as being yourselves also in the body.** 'Whereas, therefore, ye are yet in the *same state of natural life* with them, equally exposed unto all the sufferings which they undergo, be they of what kind they will, and have no assurance that ye shall be always exempted from them, this ought to be a motive unto you to be mindful of them in their present sufferings.' (John Owen) [1 *Cor* 12:25, 26]

*V*4: **Marriage is honourable in all, and the bed undefiled: but whoremongers and adulterers God will judge.**

**Let marriage be had in honour among all, and let the bed be undefiled:** (RV) Having mentioned the body, the writer goes on to enforce the sanctity of the marriage bond. This is not a statement defending marriage against a false asceticism as the AV wrongly suggests, but a serious warning not to indulge in any sexual relationship outside that honourable estate. Since sin entered the world human society always has been permissive, but Christians have been rescued from this degradation by the amazing grace of God. [cf. 1 *Cor* 6: 9–11]

**for fornicators and adulterers God will judge.** (RV) 'Most whoremongers escape human tribunals; but God takes cognizance of those whom man does not punish. Gay immoralities

will be regarded very differently from what they are now.'
(A. R. Fausset)

*V*5: **Let your conversation be without covetousness; and
be content with such things as ye have: for he hath
said, I will never leave thee, nor forsake thee.**

**Let your turn of mind be free from the love of money;**
(RV margin) 'Lust and lucre follow one another as closely
akin, both seducing the heart from the Creator to the creature.' (A. R. Fausset) [*Matt* 6: 19–21; 1 *Tim* 6:10]

**content with such things as ye have:** (RV) 'This contentment is not at all inconsistent with a duly regulated desire to
improve our circumstances, and the use of the lawful means
fitted for obtaining this purpose. It does not consist in a slothful neglect of the business of life, or a real or pretended apathy
to worldly interests. It is substantially a satisfaction with God
as our portion, and with what He is pleased to appoint for us.
It is opposed to covetousness, or the inordinate desire of
wealth; and to unbelieving anxiety – dissatisfaction with what
is present, distrust as to what is future.' (John Brown) [1 *Tim*
6:6–8]

**for himself hath said, I will in no wise fail thee, neither
will I in any wise forsake thee.** (RV) 'God's promise is better than any bond or note on any bank, financial institution,
or most stable government, for all these may have to repudiate
their bond; God never does so.' (Lenski) [*Josh* 1:5]

*V*6: **So that we may boldly say, The Lord is my helper,
and I will not fear what man shall do unto me.**

**So that with good courage we say, The Lord is my
helper; I will not fear: What shall man do unto me?**
(RV) Faith's response to the promise of the previous verse is
expressed by this quotation of *Psalm* 118:6. 'If HE has said, I
will never leave, WE may well say, What shall MAN do?'

(John Brown) [cf. *Rom* 8:31 f.] Calvin points out that as the lack of faith is the source of greed, so faith is the sovereign antidote to covetousness. 'Anyone who has the firm conviction that he will never be forsaken by the Lord will not be unduly anxious, because he will depend on His providence. Therefore when the apostle wants to cure us of the disease of greed he properly recalls us to the promises of God by which He bears witness that He will always be present to us. From this he concludes that as long as we have such a helper there is no cause for fear.' [*Matt* 6:30-34]

*V7*: **Remember them which have the rule over you, who have spoken unto you the word of God: whose faith follow, considering the end of their conversation.**

The closing appeal makes it clear that fidelity to Christ demands a final break with Judaism and involves the bearing of His reproach outside the camp. (*vv* 7-17)

**Remember them that had the rule over you, which spake unto you the word of God;** (RV) 'There would be no meaning in exhorting the Hebrews to remember their former teachers unless the exhortation were an indirect way of exhorting them not to swerve from the faith in the form in which those departed teachers had delivered it to them.' (A. B. Davidson)

**and considering the issue of their manner of life, imitate their faith.** (RV margin) A consideration of the end of their pilgrimage provides the grand incentive to imitate their faith. The Hebrews cannot expect to finish their earthly course in the same way except as they abide in the same faith. Although these leaders died in the faith they had so long confessed, there is no need to assume that they also died as martyrs for it, as some have suggested.

*V*8: **Jesus Christ the same yesterday, and today, and for ever.**

**Jesus Christ is the same yesterday and to-day, yea and for ever.** (RV) The verse affirms that Jesus Christ is still the same today as He was yesterday declared to be by their former teachers, and that He will remain the same throughout eternity. This declaration of an unchanging Christ is therefore a summons to an unchangeable faith in Him. Hence Trapp remarks, 'This was the sum of their sermons, and is the substance of their and your faith; which therefore you must stick to, standing fast in the street which is called Straight, *Acts* 9:11, and not whirred about with divers and strange doctrines.'

*V*9: **Be not carried about with divers and strange doctrines. For it is a good thing that the heart be established with grace; not with meats, which have not profited them that have been occupied therein.**

**Be not carried away by divers and strange teachings:** (RV) 'He calls the teachings which lead us away from Christ *diverse*, since there is no other simple and pure truth than the knowledge of Christ. He calls them *strange*, since God does not regard as His anything that is outside Christ. By this we are warned how we should proceed if we want to attain due proficiency in Scripture, for anyone who does not take a straight course to Christ is a wanderer.' (Calvin)

**for it is good that the heart be stablished by grace;** (RV) Their hearts cannot be made firm without their determined adherence to the doctrine they had already received, because the gospel is the sole channel through which the saving grace of God is mediated to mankind.

**not by meats, wherein they that walked were not profited.** (RV margin) Since the meticulous observance of such distinctions did not profit those who practised them, it would be sheer folly to exchange the principle of grace for the empty ritual of a vanished order. As the writer goes on to say 'we have an altar,' the term 'meats' almost certainly refers to the priestly privilege of partaking in those sacred meals which were provided by meat which had been first offered in sacrifice. 'The Apostle refers to "teachings," not to practices; it is not implied that the Hebrews were in a locality where the practices were carried on, they were being carried aside by the doctrines.' (A. B. Davidson)

*V*10: **We have an altar, whereof they have no right to eat which serve the tabernacle.**

Although Christians do not have a visible altar on which many kinds of sacrifices are offered, this does not mean that they are without an altar of their own. This 'altar' is Christ's once-for-all sacrifice which fulfilled what was foreshadowed on the Day of Atonement. On that occasion no part of the offering was reserved for the priests, for after the High Priest had presented the blood within the sanctuary, the bodies of the beasts were burned outside the camp. [*Lev* 16:27] Accordingly those who continue to 'serve the tabernacle' thereby debar themselves from any part in the offering of Christ. The benefits which Christ purchased for His people by His death cannot be enjoyed by those who remain inside the camp which crucified the Lord of glory! The observations of John Owen on this verse have lost none of their force over the years, and they are as pertinent today as when they were first written.

'*Obs*. I. That the Lord Christ, in the one sacrifice of himself, is the only altar of the church of the new testament.

*Obs*. II. That this altar is every way sufficient in itself for the end of an altar, namely, the sanctification of the people; as verse 12.

*Obs*. III. The erection of any other altar in the church, or the introduction of any other sacrifice requiring a material altar, is derogatory to the sacrifice of Christ, and exclusive of him from being our altar.'

*V11:* **For the bodies of those beasts, whose blood is brought into the sanctuary by the high priest for sin, are burned without the camp.**

*V12:* **Wherefore Jesus also, that he might sanctify the people with his own blood, suffered without the gate.**

It was because all the sins of the congregation were laid upon the bodies of these beasts that they were devoted to destruction outside the camp. In the same way Christ the sinless One became an outcast when the sins of His people were laid to His account, and He suffered outside the gate in order to exhaust the curse He bore for them. It was this vicarious bearing of the curse of sin which effected the sanctification of those He represented. Moreover, this suffering not only served to separate a people unto Himself, it also finally severed His connection with an apostate nation. 'When the Lord Jesus carried all the sins of his own people in his own body unto the tree, he left the city, as a type of all unbelievers, under the wrath and curse of God.' (John Owen)

*V13:* **Let us go forth therefore unto him without the camp, bearing his reproach.**

*V14:* **For here have we no continuing city, but we seek one to come.**

The climax of the epistle is reached in this moving appeal. No place remains for the Hebrews within the city which had rejected and crucified their Lord. They must abandon the rites and ceremonies from which the glory had departed in order to join Christ outside the camp, for it is impossible to evade bearing His reproach without also losing His presence. [*Luke* 9:23; *Phil* 3:4–10; *Heb* 11:26] Furthermore, any reluctance to renounce the protection of those religious privileges which were centred upon an earthly city would be dispelled by remembering that their real security lay in remaining faithful to their heavenly calling. 'The main business of believers in this world is diligently to seek after the city of God, or the attainment of eternal rest with him; and this is the character whereby they may be known.' (John Owen) [*Phil* 3:20; *Heb* 11:10, 13–16]

*V15*: **By him therefore let us offer the sacrifice of praise to God continually, that is, the fruit of our lips giving thanks to his name.**

John Owen notes that the next three verses give a summary of Christian duty under three heads: *Spiritual*, with respect to God, *v* 15; *Moral*, with respect to men, *v* 16; and *Ecclesiastical*, with respect to Christian leaders, *v* 17.

**By him therefore** 'And "by him", is the same with *by him alone*. There is a profane opinion and practice in the papal church about offering our sacrifices of prayer and praise to God by others; as by saints and angels, especially the blessed Virgin. But are they our altar? Did they sanctify us by their blood? Did they suffer for us without the gate? Are they the high priests of the church? Have they made us priests unto God; or prepared a new and living way for our entrance unto the throne of grace? It is on account of these things that we are said to offer our sacrifice by Christ; and it is the highest blasphemy to assign them unto any other.' It therefore follows that, 'Whatever we tender unto God, and not by Christ, it hath no other acceptance with him than the sacrifice of Cain.' (John Owen)

**let us offer the sacrifice of praise to God** 'Here we are taught what is the legitimate way of worshipping God under the new covenant, which presents another striking contrast from that which obtained under the old. As our "Altar" is not one of wood or stone, brass or gold, but Christ Himself, so our "sacrifices" are not the fruits of the ground or the firstlings of our herds, but the adoration of our hearts and the devotion of our lives. The contrast, then, is between the outward and ceremonial and the inward and spiritual.' (Arthur Pink) [*Rom* 12:1, 2]

**continually,** 'In praising a creature, we may easily exceed the truth; but in praising God, we have only to go on *confessing* what He really is to us. Hence it is impossible to exceed the truth: here is *genuine* praise.' (A. R. Fausset)

**that is, the fruit of our lips giving thanks to his name.** 'Covering God's altar with the calves of our lips, *Hos* 14:3. This shall please the Lord better than an ox or bullock, that hath horns and hoofs, *Psalm* 69:31. This also is the seeker's sacrifice, *v* 32.' (Trapp) [*Ps* 50:12-15; 51:15-17]

*V*16: **But to do good and to communicate forget not: for with such sacrifices God is well pleased.**

The sincerity of their love for God will be shown by a practical concern for the needs of others. [1 *John* 3:17] As they have been careful to do this very thing in the past, so they are to maintain the same ministry in the future. [*Heb* 6:10] This fellowship is sacrificial because it involves the Christian in sharing his temporal blessings with those in need, and with such service God is well pleased. Moreover, he who has freely received, will freely give, for an experience of grace is always reflected in a life of gratitude. [*Matt* 25:35-40; *Rom* 12:13; *Gal* 6:6; *Phil* 4:18]

*V*17: **Obey them that have the rule over you, and submit yourselves: for they watch for your souls, as they that must give account, that they may do it with joy, and not with grief: for that is unprofitable for you.**

The author previously referred to the fidelity of their former leaders in the faith; now he urges them to obey their present guides. (*vv* 7, 17) The verse rings strangely in modern ears, for many today do not associate church membership with the exercise of church discipline. However, the apostles were of another mind.

**Obey them that have the rule over you, and submit yourselves:** 'It is their duty so to *obey* whilst they [the rulers] teach the things which the Lord Christ hath appointed them to teach; for unto them is their commission limited, *Matt* 28: 20: and to *submit unto their rule* whilst it is exercised in the name of Christ, according to his institution, and by the rule of the word, and not otherwise. When they depart from these, there is neither obedience nor submission due unto them.' (John Owen)

**for they watch for your souls,** 'Watching means warning at as early a time as possible, and the warned must heed – otherwise why set watchmen? Watching implies keeping oneself and others safe where danger is known to exist or where one fears its existence. Where no danger exists watching is not needed. But where safety is at stake no one but a fool takes chances. All this applies to the church in the highest degree where the safety of souls is to be guarded.' (Lenski) [*Ezek* 33: 7–9]

**as they that must give account,** 'These are *fulmina, non verba*, as Erasmus saith of a like place, *Ezek* 3:18; not words, but thunderbolts. Chrysostom (though he usually preached every day, and so excellently that it grew to a proverb, Better the sun shine not than that Chrysostom preach not, yet he) was exceedingly affected and affrighted with this dreadful passage; being ready to say with Job, "What shall I do, when God riseth up? and when he calleth to reckoning, what shall I answer?" *Job* 31:14.' (Trapp)

**that they may do it with joy, and not with grief:** For if such willingness to hear and heed is wanting, their leaders will not be able to render a joyful account of their oversight to the 'great Shepherd of the sheep.' (v 20)

**for that is unprofitable for you.** 'When it is thus, although they alone have the present burden and trouble of it, yet it is unprofitable for the people, both here and hereafter. It is, and will be so, in the discouragement of their guides, in the displeasure of Christ, and in all the severe consequents which will ensue thereon.' (John Owen) [2 *Thess* 1:7–9]

*V*18: **Pray for us: for we trust we have a good conscience, in all things willing to live honestly.**

*V*19: **But I beseech you the rather to do this, that I may be restored to you the sooner.**

In referring to himself for the first time, the author requests the prayers of his readers. 'The allusion to his purity of conduct, and strong assertion of his consciousness of it, in regard to them and all things, when he is petitioning for their prayers, implies that some suspicions may have attached to him in the minds of some of them. These suspicions would naturally refer to his great freedom in regard to Jewish practices.' (A. B. Davidson) Although he is not detained in prison (cf. *v* 23), it seems that he is engaged on some mission which hinders his return, but he hopes that he may be soon 'restored' to them. Events would prove whether it was in fact God's will that he should return to them, yet as John Owen wisely notes, prayer is not to be ruled by the secret purposes of God. 'According unto our present apprehensions of duty, we may lawfully have earnest desires after, and pray for such things as shall not come to pass.'

*V*20: **Now the God of peace, that brought again from the dead our Lord Jesus, that great shepherd of the sheep, through the blood of the everlasting covenant,**

*V21*: **Make you perfect in every good work to do his will, working in you that which is wellpleasing in his sight, through Jesus Christ; to whom be glory for ever and ever. Amen.**

Having requested prayer for himself, the author concludes with a marvellously comprehensive prayer for his readers which recapitulates the message of the entire Epistle.

**Now the God of peace, that brought again from the dead our Lord Jesus,** It is in the raising up from the dead of 'our Lord Jesus' that God is known as the 'God of peace,' because the resurrection is the proof of our reconciliation. 'Christ, as the great shepherd of the sheep, was brought into the state of death by the sentence of the law; and was thence led, recovered, and restored, by the God of peace . . . Had not the will of God been satisfied, atonement made for sin, the church sanctified, the law accomplished, and the threatenings satisfied, Christ could not have been brought again from the dead . . . The death of Christ, if he had not risen, would not have completed our redemption, we should have been "yet in our sins;" for evidence would have been given that atonement was not made. The bare resurrection of Christ, or the bringing him from the dead, would not have saved us; for so any other man may be raised by the power of God. But the bringing again of Christ from the dead, "through the blood of the everlasting covenant," is that which gives assurance of the complete redemption and salvation of the church.' (John Owen)

**that great shepherd of the sheep,** In former days Israel had been led by other shepherds, but now true peace is found only by those who heed the voice of this 'great shepherd' for He alone ever lives to guide, guard, and rule over the flock of God. [*John* 10:1–28; I *Pet* 2:25; 5:4]

**through the blood of the everlasting covenant,** The everlasting character of this covenant is guaranteed by the eternal efficacy of that blood by which it was secured. [*Heb* 9:12]

**Make you perfect in every good work to do his will,** Although by nature we are completely unfit to perform any good work, for we have neither the inclination nor the capacity to do God's will, the grace that bestows an interest in 'the blood of the everlasting covenant' enables us to do works which God accounts as good because they are the fruit of our union with Christ ('*through* Jesus Christ'). [*Eph* 2:10]

**working in you that which is wellpleasing in his sight,** 'Whatever good we *do*, God *does* in us [*Phil* 2:13].' (A. R. Fausset)

**through Jesus Christ; to whom be the glory for ever and ever. Amen.** (RV) 'Thus shall the whole dispensation of grace issue in the eternal glory of Christ. This the Father designed; this is the blessedness of the church to give unto him, and behold; and let every one who says not amen hereunto, be *anathema Maran-atha*.' (John Owen) [I *Cor* 16:22]

*V*22: **And I beseech you, brethren, suffer the word of exhortation: for I have written a letter unto you in few words.**

What follows his prayer is in the nature of a postscript. First he urges them to 'suffer the word of exhortation' even though it should cut across their most cherished prejudices. 'Sharp though it be, and to the flesh tiresome, yet suffer it. Better it is that the vine should bleed than die. But many are like the nettle, touch it never so gently, it will sting you.' (Trapp)

**for I have written a letter unto you in few words.** 'It is reasonable to suppose that the writer means to say that he had written briefly, considering the importance and difficulty of the subjects of which he had treated. And who will deny this?' (Stuart, cited by Brown)

*V23*: **Know ye that our brother Timothy is set at liberty; with whom, if he come shortly, I will see you.**

Next he informs them of the release of Timothy with whom he hopes to visit them, provided Timothy arrives before he is obliged to start his journey. All 'that we can infer from this reference to an imprisonment of Timothy of which we have no other information is that probably the readers and certainly "the writer stood in some relationship to the Pauline world-mission circle."' (F. F. Bruce)

*V24*: **Salute all them that have the rule over you, and all the saints. They of Italy salute you.**

*V25*: **Grace be with you all. Amen.**

The usual Christian greetings and the benediction bring the Epistle to a close. It is quite impossible to determine either the location of the writer or that of the readers from the ambiguous reference to those of Italy. The benediction is identical to that found in Titus. And it is this word 'grace' which sums up all the blessings of that new and better covenant of which Jesus Christ is the divine Mediator.

## SOLI DEO GLORIA

# BIBLIOGRAPHY

Arndt, W. F.-Gingrich, F. W. *A Greek-English Lexicon of the N.T.*
    [University of Chicago Press]
Allis, O. T. *Prophecy and the Church* [P & R]
Berkhof, L. *Systematic Theology* [B of T]
Boettner, L. *Roman Catholicism* [B of T]
Bridges, C. *Commentary on Proverbs* [B of T]
Brooks, T. *Precious Remedies Against Satan's Devices* [B of T]
Brown, J. *Commentary on Hebrews* [B of T]
Bruce, F. F. *Commentary on Hebrews* [NICNT] [MMS]
Buchanan, J. *The Doctrine of Justification* [B of T]
Burroughs, J. *The Rare Jewel of Christian Contentment* [B of T]
Calvin, J. *Commentary on Genesis* [B of T]
Calvin, J. *Commentary on Hebrews* [O & B]
Cunningham, W. *Historical Theology* [B of T]
Davidson, A. B. *Hebrews* [HBC] [T & T Clark]
Denney, J. *The Death of Christ* [Tyndale]
Fausset, A. R. *Hebrews* [JFB] [Eerdmans]
Flavel, J. *Works, Vols. I & III* [B of T]
Hammond, T. C. *The One Hundred Texts* [MMS]
Henry, M. *Commentary on the Bible* [MMS]
Hewitt, T. *Hebrews* [TNTC] [Tyndale]
Hodge, C. *Commentary on I Corinthians* [B of T]
Kuyper, A. *The Work of the Holy Spirit* [Eerdmans]
Lenski, R. C. H. *The Interpretation of the Epistle to the Hebrews*
    [Augsburg]
Lightfoot, J. B. *Commentary on Colossians and Philemon* [Zondervan]
Lightfoot, J. B. *Commentary on Philippians* [Zondervan]

Machen, J. G. *The Christian View of Man* [B of T]

Manson, W. *The Epistle to the Hebrews* [H & S]

Murray, J. *The Covenant of Grace* [Tyndale]

Murray, J. *Commentary on Romans* [NICNT] [MMS]

Murray, J. *Redemption Accomplished and Applied* [B of T]

North, Brownlow *The Rich Man and Lazarus* [B of T]

Owen, J. *An Exposition of Hebrews* [SGP]

Owen, J. *Works, Vol. VII* [B of T]

Palmer, S. *The Nonconformist's Catechism (Sermons of the Great Ejection)* [B of T]

Pink, A. *Exposition of Hebrews* [Baker]

Poole, M. *Commentary on the Holy Bible, Vol. III* [B of T]

Ridderbos, H. *The Coming of the Kingdom* [P & R]

Smeaton, G. *The Apostles' Doctrine of the Atonement* [Zondervan]

Smeaton, G. *The Doctrine of the Holy Spirit* [B of T]

Souter, A. *A Pocket Lexicon to the Greek N.T.* [Oxford]

Stibbs, A. M. *The Finished Work of Christ* [Tyndale]

Stibbs, A. M. *The Meaning of the Word 'Blood' in Scripture* [Tyndale]

Stibbs, A. M. *Commentary on Hebrews* [NBC] [IVP]

Stonehouse, N. B. (contributor to) *The Infallible Word* [P & R]

Tasker, R. V. G. *The Gospel in the Epistle to the Hebrews* [Tyndale]

Trapp, J. *Commentary on the N.T.* [SGP]

Trench, R. C. *Synonyms of the N.T.* [James Clarke]

Venning, R. *The Plague of Plagues* [B of T]

Vine, W. E. *Expository Dictionary of N.T. Words* [Oliphants]

Vos, G. *Biblical Theology* [Eerdmans]

Vos, G. *The Self-Disclosure of Jesus* [Eerdmans]

Vos, G. *The Teaching of the Epistle to the Hebrews* [Eerdmans]

Warfield, B. B. *Biblical and Theological Studies* [P & R]

Warfield, B. B. *The Inspiration and Authority of the Bible* [MMS]

Warfield, B. B. *Miracles: Yesterday and Today, Real and Counterfeit* [P & R]

Wuest, K. *Hebrews in the Greek N.T.* [P & I]

Wyngaarden, M. *The Future of the Kingdom in Prophecy & Fulfilment* [Baker]

Young, E. J. *Thy Word is Truth* [B of T]